Hamlyn all-colour paperbacks

Charles Chilton

Discovery of the
American West

illustrated by Michael McGuinness

Hamlyn · London
Sun Books · Melbourne

FOREWORD

The Discovery of the American West tells the story of the expansion
of the American frontier from the War of Independence to the final
conquest and subjugation of the whole territory now forming the
United States.

The 'West' of the nineteenth century was not a specified area
with fixed boundaries and a uniform topography. During the great
migration from the Atlantic seaboard towards the Pacific, spread
over roughly a hundred years, the 'West' meant something different
to each successive wave of settlers.

To the early colonists the 'West' meant the land that lay immediately beyond the Appalachian Mountains. The next natural
barrier was the 'great plains' area, originally known as the 'great
American desert'. The 'West' then became the area that lay beyond
the Rocky Mountains and the Sierra Nevada. These ranges had to be
conquered before the glittering prizes of California and Oregon
could be won.

Besides these natural hazards, all American pioneers had to face
resistance to their advance from other races; French, Spanish,
Mexican and, above all, Indians. In *The Discovery of the American
West* I have tried to show how these obstacles were overcome and
to tell something of the different ways of life which evolved in the
process.

Charles Chilton.

Published by The Hamlyn Publishing Group Limited
London · New York · Sydney · Toronto
Hamlyn House, Feltham, Middlesex, England
In association with Sun Books Pty Ltd Melbourne

Copyright © The Hamlyn Publishing Group Limited 1970

SBN 600 00278 0
Phototypeset by BAS Printers Limited, Wallop, Hampshire
Colour separations by Schwitter Limited, Zurich
Printed in England by Sir Joseph Causton & Sons Limited

CONTENTS

THE WILDERNESS ROAD

To the original thirteen British colonies established on the Atlantic coast of North America, the first 'American West' was the land hidden from their view and experience by the Appalachians.

The pioneers of westward expansion were the fur traders. The French, who laid claim to the huge regions from the Alleghenies to the Rockies and from Lake Superior to the Gulf of Mexico, had established a very profitable trade with the Indians.

New immigrants from Britain found it profitable to build their homes along the western fringe of the older communities Soon they were looking longingly at the vast expanse of the lands beyond the mountains. Land companies were formed to explore and locate suitable territories for settlement; the Ohio Land Company in 1747; the Loyal Land Company in 1749.

Alarmed at these intrusions into their territory the French constructed a series of forts stretching from Lake Erie to the

The USA at the time of independence (1783)

Ohio River. By 1754 the 'French and Indian War', an undeclared conflict and a prelude to the Seven Years War between France and Britain had begun.

By the treaty of Paris, 1763, when France was finally defeated, all Canada and all land east of the Mississippi River passed under British rule. Now, thought the energetic British colonists, the long-awaited mass move to the far west beyond the Appalachians could begin.

But in May 1763, came the 'Pontiac Conspiracy' when the Ottawa Indian chief led his warriors in a bloody uprising against British outposts and slaughtered hundreds of British subjects. The British government, already tired and exhausted by the long wars, decided to appease the Indians.

The colonists were bitterly disappointed, especially as some colonial governors had promised lands beyond the mountains to volunteers who had served in the colonial armies. Now, it seemed, such lands were to be barred to them for ever.

But the British government found itself powerless to stop the westward movement. As early as 1750 Dr Thomas

Indians attack farmers

Cumberland Gap, a natural mountain pass discovered in 1750

Walker of the Loyal Land Company had led a surveying party across the Appalachians into the fertile land of Kentucky. He named the pass through which he traversed the mountains 'Cumberland Gap' in honour of the Duke of Cumberland. Although expansion of white settlement continued along the whole length of the frontier it was in this central area where the valley of western Virginia stretches towards Cumberland Gap that the pressure was greatest. A new breed of men had grown up in this region; men who had lived all their lives on the untamed frontier. Hunting to them was the natural way of life. Their favourite weapon was the long rifle. They were expert marksmen. They totally ignored the proclamation of 1763 and continued to hunt and explore where they liked. They were known as the 'long hunters' because of the great distances they travelled, usually on foot. Typical of this new breed was Daniel Boone.

On 1 May 1769, Boone and a party of long hunters passed through the Cumberland Gap into central Kentucky. They explored much of the territory before returning home. Boone, however, remained behind and lived alone in the great forest for nearly two years while he explored the rivers and enjoyed the freedom of the woods. He must also have been on the lookout for good land on which to settle for, in 1773, he decided to move his family into the new territory.

With six other families he began the laborious process of transporting women, children, household goods and livestock up the tortuous and muddy trail known as the Wilderness Road. But attacks by Indians drove them back and the project failed.

Two years later, in January 1775, Boone again headed for the Gap. This time he led his party through it and on to the south bank of the Kentucky River. There he founded a settlement later known as Boonesborough.

By May that year there were three settlements in Kentucky. All of them had defied the British proclamation prohibiting expansion into Indian territory. But by then the Revolutionary War was in full swing. When it was over the American colonists had gained their independence and no longer felt bound by any British treaty with the Indians.

Daniel Boone

Marylanders heading west

Now the pioneers, poised on the edge of the Appalachians, rolled forward to fill up the great area east of the Mississippi. In 1775 there had been an estimated population of 100 persons in Kentucky; by 1784 there were 30,000. Men looking for cheap land and new opportunity now set forth in thousands from the middle states to seek new homes in the west.

Later, as the rough trails grew wider, the emigrants piled their homes into covered wagons drawn by slow-plodding oxen.

Some, instead of taking the Wilderness Road to the south took the old Braddock Road to Pittsburg. There a family could acquire a large raft or 'flat boat' on which they could float themselves and their belongings down the Allegheny to the Ohio.

The land which the settlers were entering was fertile, well watered and heavily timbered. With the abundant timber log cabins were quickly and easily constructed. The axe played as large a part as the rifle in the immigrant's new life. The forests had to be cut down before crops could be planted or stock raised. Maize, wheat, oats, barley and rye all flourished; fruit trees, particularly apples did well. Cattle and hogs thrived in the valleys.

By 1792 Kentucky had become a state. Tennessee followed in 1796 and Ohio in 1803. To the south and west of these states stretched the great area known as Louisiana Territory which, although formerly French, had been ceded to Spain in 1762. In 1800, Spain ceded Louisiana back to France and in 1803 Napoleon, who needed money to pay for his wars against England, sold it to the United States for eighty million francs. With the purchase of Louisiana the land area of the United States was virtually doubled. Enough land had been acquired to form thirteen new states. Kentucky, Tennessee and Ohio were, suddenly, the 'West' no longer.

Immigrant chopping timber to build a log cabin

BLAZING THE TRAILS

The boundaries of Louisiana had never been very precise. The American Government did not know the exact limit of the area it had purchased. When the north-west boundary was later in dispute with Great Britain the United States actually claimed the area now forming the states of Oregon, Washington and Idaho as part of the Louisiana Purchase. In fact the purchase did not include any land west of the Rocky Mountains or south of the Red River; the area which forms the present day states of California, Nevada, Utah, Colorado, Arizona, New Mexico and Texas remained in Spanish hands.

Nevertheless the purchase of the new territory, known at first as the District of Louisiana and later divided into Louisiana and Missouri Territories, opened the way for American occupation of the whole of what is now known as 'The West'.

Now that New Orleans had become an American port the Mississippi became an increasingly important trade route for the products of western settlements and an assured outlet for their produce was a great inducement to migrant farmers.

The Louisiana Purchase was negotiated with France in 1803

Lewis and Clark — their expedit on opened up vast new territories to knowledge

As a result of the Purchase, a whole new area was also opened up to the fur traders who now increasingly explored the upper reaches of the Mississippi and its tributary the Missouri. But the most important development in the history of the far west at this time was the decision of the United States Government to send out official expeditions to survey the newly acquired territory.

Thomas Jefferson, who became President of the United States in 1801, well understood the importance of exploring the territory west of the Mississippi. He was particularly anxious to discover a river passage to the north-west coast where Americans and British were already carrying on a rival trade in sea otter furs.

The first expedition he organized was led by his private secretary, Captain Meriwether Lewis, with Lieutenant William Clark as his second-in-command.

The expedition was instructed to chart all rivers, islands and unusual landmarks, to contact and observe Indian tribes, their locations, manners and customs; and to record animal plant and insect life. The time allocated for the journey — expected to be roughly 4,000 miles — was two years.

On 4 May 1804, Lewis and Clark set off from St Louis, the capital of Upper Louisiana. The forty-five members of the expedition, which included fourteen serving soldiers, two Frenchmen and a Negro slave, travelled in three boats. The first part of the journey took them up the Missouri to the villages of the Mandan Indians where they spent the winter.

When the thaw came in the spring they moved on. They had no idea what lay ahead of them. They passed through treeless undulating prairie country on which they saw great herds of buffalo; they hunted and collected specimens, drew maps and kept diaries. On 13 June 1805, they came upon the Great Falls of the Missouri. To get round them they had to make a 'portage' of some eighteen miles carrying all their equipment and boats on their backs. The Rocky Mountains were reached on 20 July.

Now began the worst part of the journey. Shoshone Indians guided them on foot through the high mountains where game was nonexistent. They were reduced to living on berries, roots and dried fish. In the high altitude it

Mandan Village — Lewis and Clark wintered in one, 1804—5

was very cold. There was a danger that winter would overtake them whilst they were still crossing the summits. At last on 7 October they sighted the south fork of the Clearwater River. They halted to build canoes and then floated down the Clearwater to the Snake. At last, on 7 November, they sighted the Pacific Ocean.

The return journey began in March 1806. On 29 June they reached Travellers Rest Creek where the party split up. Lewis crossed the Divide by the Shoshone 'buffalo trail' while Clark went south and explored the Yellowstone river. They met again some 200 miles west of the Mandan villages on the Missouri and arrived back at St Louis on 23 September.

The journey of Lewis and Clark was remarkable from many aspects. It was the first organized attempt to penetrate the mysterious 'Far West' which had been the subject of much rumour and speculation. Their reports made Americans realize the extent and possibilities of their newly acquired territory. Lewis and Clark laid the foundation of the Oregon Trail along which thousands of emigrants were later to travel.

Buffalo

While Lewis and Clark were exploring the north-west, another expedition, led by Lieutenant Zebulon Montgomery Pike, set off from St Louis, ostensibly to explore the Red River and determine its source. Pike travelled due west along the Missouri until he reached the fork called the Osage river. The Osage, like most western rivers, proved impracticable for canoes. The expedition continued on horseback, across the great plains of Kansas and Colorado. Like the Spaniards before him and the travellers who came after him, Pike was awed and bewildered by the great open spaces. He suffered all the hazards of travel on the plains; heat, cold, loss of direction and attacks by hostile Indians. Eventually he, too, saw the Rocky Mountains with one peak in particular soaring high above him. This peak he climbed and explored. Later it was to bear his name and to become a landmark for gold seekers and other travellers to California.

In the mountains Pike spent many miserable months searching for the source of the Red River. He suffered terribly from the cold. But after crossing the Sangre de

Zebulon Pike, the American explorer

Cristo Mountains the party found a small river which
they thought to be the Red. They built a stockade on its
banks. But soon Pike was arrested by a party of Spanish
cavalry. They informed the lieutenant that he was trespassing
on Spanish territory and took him to Santa Fe.

Some historians believe that Pike deliberately let himself
be captured. Spain viewed the westward expansion of the
United States with great apprehension. She had already
closed all Spanish trails to American traders, except in
Mexico. By being taken to Santa Fe Pike was able to observe
at first hand Spanish possessions which till then had been
shrouded in mystery. When, after courteous treatment, he
was released and returned to US territory, Pike's copious
notes made interesting reading for the government.

Pike had hardly made his report before American traders
began to forsake the old trail down to Santa Cruz in Mexico
and take to the Santa Fe trail instead. But it was not until
1821 when Mexico won its independence from Spain that
the Santa Fe trade really got under way.

15

In that year a trader named William Becknell succeeded in reaching Santa Fe with a pack train. He sold his goods at five times their worth in St Louis. By 1824 eight traders had followed his example and were engaged in a flourishing trade with the Mexicans.

Goods for Santa Fe were shipped along the Missouri river as far as Independence where they were loaded into wagons or on to pack mules. From Independence the trail crossed to the great bend of the Arkansas and then led to the Cimarron. The stretch of desert between these two rivers was the most dreaded part of the road. Scorching heat, lack of water, sand storms and Indian attacks were only a few of the hazards to be faced.

From the Cimarron River the trail passed to the headwaters of the Canadian and the Pecos rivers in the Sangre de Cristo range. Once through the mountains the sleepy town of Santa Fe could be seen lying on the plain beyond. More trouble lay in wait for the wagoners as they descended the slopes towards their goal. Mexican bandits lay waiting to

Santa Fe in New Mexico is the oldest capital city in the U.S.

Mountain man

ambush the caravans.

In 1843 the monetary return from trade with Santa Fe was reckoned to be 450,000 dollars. But the Mexican authorities grew alarmed at the increasing flow of Americans into their territory and finally put a stop to the trade. The Santa Fe 'bullwhackers' had to turn to other fields.

With the opening of the Santa Fe Trail, fur traders became active in and around the district. Their headquarters was at nearby Taos where whole 'brigades' of 'mountain men', as the fur traders were called, met to barter their wares with Indians and Mexicans.

In 1826 a young lad who had joined one of the most famous companies then operating on the Santa Fe Trail – the Bent Brothers – left the caravan and journeyed to Taos determined to become a 'mountain man'. His name was Christopher Carson, later to be known throughout the west as 'Kit' Carson. As a member of Ewing Young's fur trapping brigade he learnt all there was to be known about beaver trapping, buffalo hunting, tracking and Indian fighting. Later he formed his own company of guides and scouts. 'Carson's Men' were hired by all kinds of expeditions throughout the west. Kit Carson himself was to guide John Charles Fremont

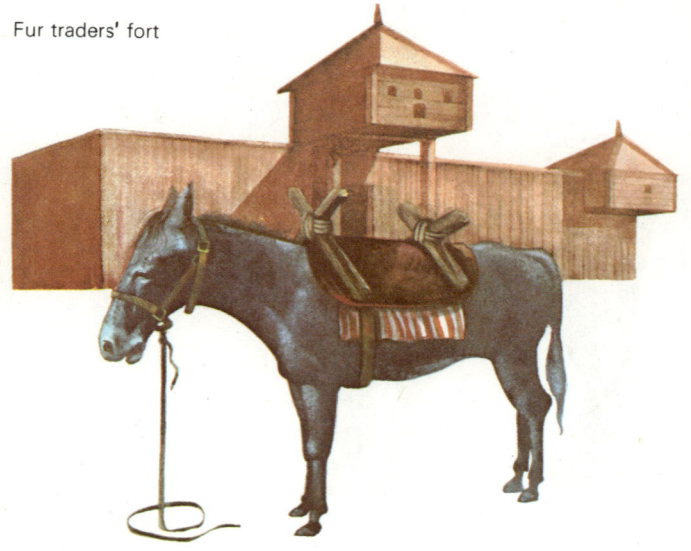

on his expeditions to California which were to result in yet another advance of the United States' western frontier towards the Pacific.

Fur trading west of the Mississippi led to the discovery of new passes through the Rocky Mountains and to the exploration of the unknown land beyond.

Two companies dominated the fur trade in this area; the American Fur Company, founded in 1808 by John Jacob Astor, and the Rocky Mountain Fur Company founded in 1822 by General W. H. Ashley.

The American Fur Company followed the course of the rivers and built permanent outposts along their banks. At these outposts, which were strongly fortified, Indians traded their pelts for beads, blankets, cloth, mirrors, alcohol, guns and powder. The line of forts followed the route taken by Lewis and Clark.

The Rocky Mountain Fur Company did not depend on Indians to bring pelts to forts. Instead it sent its own brigades of white trappers *overland* into the mountains to collect furs and bring them each year to a pre-arranged 'rendezvous'.

Trapping beaver

Beaver hat

Throughout the spring and early summer the hunters travelled in small groups setting their traps. At the end of the season they took their pelts to the rendezvous from where transport parties carried them back to St Louis by pack train. The annual rendezvous was a festive occasion in which trappers and traders indulged themselves in an orgy of eating and drinking – especially drinking.

Among the mountain men were some of the most skilled and courageous trappers of the west; men like Jedediah Smith and Jim Bridger who, in their search for furs, also made considerable additions to geographical knowledge. Jim Bridger was the first white man to hunt along the shores of the Great Salt Lake; Jedediah Smith discovered two passes through the mighty Sierra Nevada range. But the greatest achievement of the Rocky Mountain Fur Company was to discover South Pass. The discovery of this Rocky Mountain pass, which was some twenty miles wide and reached by a comparatively gradual ascent, opened up a central trans-continental route suitable for wagon trains. It was to become the gateway to California.

19

Treaty with Blackfeet Indians

Lewis and Clark got on well with the Indians they met. They treated them with respect and fairness and in consequence secured the friendship of such tribes as the Nez Percé and the Flatheads. These Indians never molested the white immigrants who followed the Lewis and Clark trail. But the fierce Blackfeet Indians of the north-west resented the intrusion of white men into their hunting grounds. They were determined to keep the white men out. If a trapper entered their lands he did so at his peril. The American Fur Company's outposts were in constant danger of attack as were the pack trains of the Rocky Mountain Fur Company.

In 1830, Kenneth MacKenzie of the American Fur Company succeeded in making a trade treaty with the Blackfeet. He built an outpost deep in their country and bribed the Indians to deal only with him. In so doing he obtained access to a vast supply of furs and became allied with a tribe which continued to wage war on his rivals.

MacKenzie also aped the practice of the Rocky Mountain boys and sent trappers into the mountains. Pitched battles broke out between trappers of the two companies; eventually a regular 'fur war' ensued. Unfortunately for its rival, the American Fur Company had the strong backing of financial interests in the east. The Rocky Mountain Fur Company was virtually self supporting. In 1834, unable to compete with its richer rival, it collapsed. Ten years later the fur trade itself died. The beaver hat, for years the main support of the American fur trade, went out of fashion and was replaced by the new, silk top hat. The bottom dropped out of the beaver market.

But the mountain men's experience as trappers and explorers stood them and the country in good stead. Even before the collapse of the fur trade, emigrant trains were moving westward across the Rockies. For safety's sake these trains needed guides, scouts and wagon masters. They found them among the men who had blazed the very trails they were using. So, instead of trapping furs, mountain men now earned a living by leading settlers across the Rockies to new homes in Oregon or conducting prospectors to the gold fields of California.

Trappers : a misunderstanding

Ownership of the mountainous, timbered territory which now forms the state of Oregon in the extreme north-western corner of the United States was in dispute for many years. Soon after the Lewis and Clark expedition the American Fur Company established a fort – Astoria – on the mouth of the Columbia. But after the war of 1812 British influence predominated. The British Hudson Bay Company secured a monopoly of the fur trade in the area.

Then, in 1831, four Flathead Indians arrived at St Louis asking for Christian missionaries to be sent to their country in the north-west. It is not clear what prompted the Flatheads to do this. Possibly they had been influenced by trappers like Jedediah Smith who was a Presbyterian and a very religious man; in any case, it was the Methodists who answered the Indians' call. In 1833, two missionaries, Jason and Daniel Lee, left New York, travelled up the Missouri to Independence and joined a fur trading pack train on its way up the Platte river. On 28 April 1834, they arrived at Fort Vancouver.

In 1838 Jason Lee travelled back to the east to seek funds

The first emigrant train through Scott's Bluff

Flathead Indian

for his mission. His lectures about this new land far to the north-west were heard by many frontier families living on the edge of the great plains. They liked his descriptions of the wooded, well-watered valleys and hills. As a result, in May 1841, the first party to head for Oregon was formed at Sapling Grove, Missouri.

By 1846 the trickle of emigrants had become a flood. Soon there were so many Americans in the area that its annexation by the United States was inevitable. 'Our title to the country of Oregon', stated President Polk, 'is clear and unquestionable . . . Our people have adventurously ascended the Missouri to its head springs and are already engaged in establishing the blessings of self-government.'

'Manifest Destiny' – the belief fixed in the minds of pioneers that they served a national destiny as they pressed westward – was the political slogan. 'Fifty-four Forty or Fight!' screamed the expansionists. By the treaty of 1846 the present boundary was fixed. Britain retained Vancouver Island, but the United States received title to all land to the south of it.

The camp meeting was a communal service for settlers

WESTWARD WITH GOD

The pioneer families who journeyed along the rivers or the wilderness road to seek new homes in the west were not a godless people but, because settlements were scattered and towns scarce, few churches were built.

Various denominations, chiefly the Presbyterians, Methodists and Baptists, anxious that the settlers should not lose touch with God, sent missionaries into the wilderness. They travelled on horseback, but it took weeks for a single preacher to get round to holding services for all the isolated families in just one area.

A solution to this problem was found in the 'camp meeting'. Instead of preachers riding circuit they announced that a religious meeting would be held at a certain place and time. Settlers, sometimes from a hundred miles around or more, would ride to the rendezvous. There they would camp in tents or in the backs of their wagons. Hence the name 'Camp Meeting'.

Around 1800 a great spiritual 'awakening' took place along the frontier. It began in Kentucky where, at Cane Ridge, 25,000 settlers of all Protestant denominations took part in a great revival meeting. The preachers, with their fiery sermons on sin, hell-fire and salvation worked their listeners into a state of near-hysteria.

Out of this emotional, boisterous, religious fervour many new sects were born: among them were the Campbellites, the Millerites, the Oneida Colony and the Shakers. From the point of view of westward expansion, however, the most important of the new sects was the 'Church of Jesus Christ of the Latter-Day Saints' whose followers became known as 'Mormons'. Joseph Smith, the founder, claimed that the fullness of the Gospel was made known to him by an angel named Moroni who revealed to Smith the book of the prophet Mormon. With its aid and by divine authority Smith was to re-establish the Church of Jesus Christ on earth.

Smith and his disciples, by their persuasive oratory and burning zeal and energy, attracted many followers in New

Emigrant ship

York State where the new church was officially inaugurated on 6 June 1830. However the Mormons soon found themselves subjected to so much criticism, ridicule and antagonism that Smith decided to move his people to a more tolerant frontier community. The place he chose was Kirtland, Ohio. In 1831 the Mormons began their first trek westwards.

No sooner had they established themselves in Kirtland than the increasing flow of 'Gentile' immigrants brought fresh persecutions, tarring and feathering and other indignities. So the Mormons moved on to Independence in Missouri and thence to a town called 'Far West'. The Mormons were detested by the average American frontiersman and they suffered almost continual persecution, yet their numbers steadily increased.

This was due to most encouraging support from converts overseas, particularly from Great Britain. Most British workers lived in appalling conditions at that time. In place of filthy slum dwellings, the Mormons offered converts sunshine, wide open spaces and fresh air.

But while the missionaries were doing such sterling work in Europe, the American Saints were again heading west and painfully making their way towards the town of Commerce, on the Mississippi River. Within four years the swampy site had been transformed into a flourishing town without equal on the American frontier. It boasted not only a temple but also a university. Its name was changed from Commerce to Nauvoo, a word from the Hebrew meaning 'beautiful'.

As well as the antagonism of isolated farmers who were jealous of the economic success the Mormon co-operative effort seemed to bring, the Mormons were surrounded by political enemies who were frightened of the influence the increasing numbers of 'Saints' might have on state politics. Even more disastrous, from the point of view of Mormon-Gentile relations, was the announcement that a 'revelation' had informed Joseph Smith that polygamy could henceforward be practised by his followers. The Mormon communities had received a remarkable influx of women converts from Europe which may have had something to do with Smith's announcement but to most 'Gentile' frontier communities where women were scarce, the idea of polygamy was abhorrent.

A violent new wave of persecutions against the Mormons began. Joseph Smith and his brother Hyram were arrested and placed in the jail at Carthage. There a section of the state militia stormed the jail, broke down the door of the room in which Smith was imprisoned and shot him dead as he tried to jump from the window.

The Mormon town of Nauvoo

Mormons crossing a frozen river

The leadership of the church was now assumed by Brigham Young. He realized that it was impossible for the Mormons to stay in Nauvoo. They would have to move. But where to? The only course, Young reckoned, was to head directly westward where no other pioneers had reached or intended to settle.

The first six hundred saints to leave Nauvoo crossed the frozen Mississippi on 4 February 1846. Small pioneer parties were sent ahead to survey the route, look for water and mark the best places for camping. The first encampment, made in bitterly cold weather, was at Sugar Creek on the west bank of the Mississippi.

As soon as the warm spring weather softened the soil, acres of ground were fenced in and broken by the plough. Crops were planted so that others following that way in the fall could reap the harvest. On the western banks of the Missouri Young established 'Winter Quarters', now Florence, Nebraska. There the saints spent the terrible winter of 1846–47. Many died of hunger and exposure.

Early in the spring of 1847 Brigham Young and 148 volunteers left Winter Quarters and travelled up the Platte River to South Pass where they turned southward to the fur trading post of Fort Bridger. Brigham Young asked Jim Bridger about the possibilities of starting an agricultural

The seagull miracle

settlement in the Great Basin country west of the Rockies. Bridger's answer was not encouraging. He was prepared to bet that no crops could be grown anywhere in that area.

In spite of Bridger's warnings the Mormons decided to cross the Rockies. In the train that wound its way slowly through the mountains Brigham Young lay sick in one of the wagons. At a look-out point on Big Mountain the train stopped. The Mormon leader sat up and looked down at the great valley lying before him. He said: 'It is enough. This is the right place. Drive on.'

During the next few weeks the saints worked themselves almost to exhaustion. The valley was dry, barren and plagued with insects. Irrigation ditches had to be dug, streams dammed and, as there were few trees, building materials had to be carried down from the mountains. Crops were planted almost immediately and temporary adobe houses built.

The first winter was grim. Food was short; wolves, mountain lions and foxes preyed on supplies and on live-stock; desert mice plagued the cabins; diseases, especially measles, claimed many victims. Nevertheless mills were built and large fields were planted with wheat in the early spring. As there was an unusual amount of rain, the wheat seemed to be doing well.

In May, however, great swarms of crickets descended on the ripening crop and began to consume it. Desperately, the Mormons battled against them, but in vain. Then, miraculously and in answer to their prayers, flocks of seagulls swooped in from the islands of the great Salt Lake and saved the wheat by eating the insects.

In 1848 more than two hundred souls arrived from Winter Quarters. The building of Salt Lake City went ahead. Brigham Young and the Elders located the site of the Temple and planned the city around it. Few cities in America were fortunate enough to be organized on such excellent lines. Brigham Young's foresight is evident in the layout of the present-day city with its wide airy streets, rows of trees and fountains of ice-cold mountain water on the street corners.

Now that the Mormons were safely established in their New Zion, missionaries abroad were instructed to encourage converts to join their brethren in the Great Salt Lake Valley. Economic conditions in Britain had been steadily deteriorat-

In 1856 1,300 Mormon converts made the journey to Salt Lake City

ing and thousands, especially from Wales, eagerly responded to the call. They were transported in special emigrant ships across the Atlantic and thence by train to Missouri. But there new difficulties arose. Few emigrants had the money to buy the necessary oxen, mules and wagons to make the hazardous journey across the plains and mountains to Salt Lake City.

An edict went out from Brigham Young's office: 'The Lord, through his Prophet, says of the poor "Let them come on foot, with hand-carts or wheel barrows, let them gird up their loins and walk through and nothing shall hinder them!"'

Hundreds of simple two-wheeled wooden vehicles were built. In May and early June 1856, the first 1,300 European converts set out to cover the journey from Iowa to Salt Lake on foot, pushing their handcarts before them. The first three handcart companies, made up of a hundred carts, with 900 men, women and children, arrived in the Salt Lake Valley late in September.

Two remaining companies, consisting mainly of English,

The handcart trek

Mormon Temple in Salt Lake City, Utah

Scots, Scandinavians and Germans ran into serious difficulties. But in spite of such suffering nearly 3,000 people
walked the 1500 miles to Salt Lake City between 1856–60.

From Salt Lake City the Mormons spread out into the
surrounding wilderness to irrigate new farms and establish
new townships. Slowly the unfertile, arid lands began to
flower and the communities to prosper. By 1849 they were
calling their territory the 'state' of Deseret, a state governed
entirely by the Mormon church. Inevitably they came into
conflict with the government in Washington. Eventually the
area became the territory of Utah with Brigham Young
appointed territorial governor. Not until 1896 when polygamy was officially abandoned did Utah become a state
within the Union.

Today Utah remains a predominantly Mormon state. The
beautiful city of Salt Lake, with its world-famous temple and
tabernacle, its wide streets, beautiful trees and flowers,
stands as a monument to those hardy trail-breakers who
planted such a tenacious community in the midst of a
territory which, before they arrived, had been called the
'great American desert'.

DOWN BY THE RIO GRANDE

After their conquest of Mexico the Spaniards had tried to extend their colonial system north of the Rio Grande River. But the fierce plains Indians were a constant menace, especially after they had learnt to use the horse.

The mounted Apaches and Comanches would not be subdued and converted as the peaceful Pueblo tribes of New Mexico and Arizona had been. They ambushed the soldiers, burned the missions and drove off the settlers' stocks of cattle and horses. By 1762 Santa Fe in New Mexico and San Antonio in Texas still remained as two outposts of the Spanish colonial empire but the attempt to advance out onto the plains had been abandoned. Many missions and ranches were deserted and their livestock left to fend for themselves. They did this so successfully that soon the land between the Nueces River and the Rio Grande, the extreme southern tip of Texas, was swarming with cattle and horses.

The Spanish now attempted to extend their frontier eastwards towards New Orleans in order to check French expansion. It was from the friendly Tejas Indians of this region that Texas got its name. After the Louisiana Purchase the boundary line between the American and Spanish possessions was a tributary of the Mississippi.

Eastern Texas was very different from the plains area further west. To American frontiersmen poised on the Mississippi it appeared an attractive, desirable land. Even before the purchase of Louisiana, a few Americans were allowed by the Spanish government to settle there.

Spanish missions north of the Rio Grande

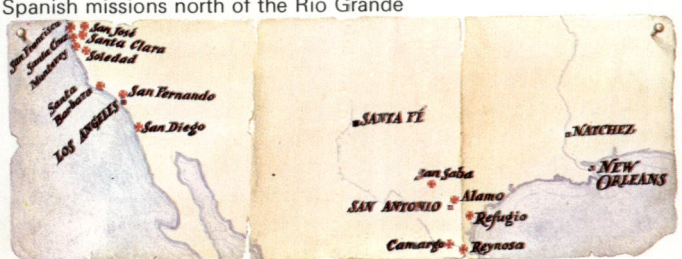

Spanish mission

In December 1820, Moses Austin, a business man who had lived in Missouri since 1798 when it still belonged to Spain, asked permission of the Spanish governor in San Antonio to establish a colony of three hundred American families in Texas. He was granted the right to organize a colony between the Colorado and the Brazos rivers.

In that same year came the Mexican revolution which threw off Spanish rule. Now the little colony of Americans was subject to Mexican legislation which in the turmoil of revolution was unstable and vacillating. Then Moses Austin died. His son, Stephen, took over the leadership of his father's settlements.

The Americans found that by declaring their intent to raise cattle the Mexican authorities granted them much larger areas of land.

Nevertheless cattle raising at this stage was no more than a sideline. The new Texans still considered themselves to be farmers. They grew cotton, corn and sweet potatoes and lived and worked much as they had done in their old homes back in Mississippi, Kentucky or Tennessee.

In 1828 there were 2,000 Americans in Austin's colonies.

By 1831 there were 5,665 and most of them lived along the well-watered and well-timbered land of the Brazos and Colorado rivers. As more and more immigrants arrived they found the only available lands were to the north, north-west or south-west. In whichever direction they travelled they came in contact with the great plains and in conflict with the plains Indians.

Austin's colony itself, though not on the plains, was near enough to experience and sometimes suffer Indian attacks. As a result it was agreed that from twenty to thirty 'rangers' should be kept in service to combat the Indians. From these small beginnings developed the famous Texas Rangers.

The Texans had soon realized that mounted Indians could not be successfully contended with on foot. As they moved nearer and nearer the plains region the horse became an all-important means of transport and fighting. This fact, together with the Spanish cattle thriving in the Nueces Valley, was to create a new breed of frontiersman and a new way of life; the Texan cowboy and the cattle industry. But before these could develop the new settlers had to obtain their independence from Mexico.

Anglo-Saxon colonists

Battle of the Alamo, fought in 1836 between the Texans and the Mexicans

The dominating motive of the frontiersman was to find land. If the land was there he saw no reason why he should not move in and claim it. When he crossed into Texas he did not stop to think what life would be like under Mexican rule. The average settler saw very little of the Mexicans and left the administration of the colony to Austin and other agents who undertook all the necessary dealings with the Mexican government.

As, however, the tide of immigration increased and Americans flooded into Texas the Mexican authorities became alarmed. If the flow was not stopped American annexation of Texas would be a *fait accompli*. On 6 April 1830, a decree was passed prohibiting further American immigration. At the same time customs duties were imposed and Mexican troops were garrisoned in Texas.

To the American settlers these impositions seemed a restriction of their freedom. The idea of paying taxes was abhorrent to any frontiersman; to have them imposed by such an 'inferior' race of people as the Mexicans and, worse still, to have Mexican troops enforcing their collection was the last straw. Amidst a vast amount of political intrigue and incitement from some of the more unruly elements who inevitably appeared in a frontier community a definite

movement towards Texas independence arose.

Among the leading men behind the move for self-government were Sam Houston, a Virginian who had once been Governor of Tennessee and James Bowie, remembered these days more for his gruesome hunting knife than for his political activities.

In 1833 Stephen Austin asked Mexico City for some measure of self-government. But in reply Santa Anna, now dictator of Mexico, dissolved the legislature and sent a military force to Gonzales to take the town's cannon before the Texans should get hold of them.

A volunteer army quickly gathered. They were mostly farmers, armed with squirrel guns, Bowie knives, kitchen knives or any other crude weapon they could lay their hands on. They gave Santa Anna's force at Gonzales a sound beating and, on 9 December 1835, took the city of San Antonio.

Santa Anna was determined to put an end to this rebellion. In March 1836, he led an army of 5,000 troops towards San Antonio. The Texans had hoped for reinforcements from the United States but they did not arrive. Therefore the town was evacuated with the exception of a rear-guard of 187 men who took refuge behind the walls of the ancient Alamo Mission. Here Travis, Bowie, Davy Crockett and their 184 companions died to the last man in an effort to block Santa Anna's march into the interior.

Sam Houston was the newly appointed commander-in-chief of the Texan army. He drew his scattered troops together as Santa Anna advanced towards the Sabine River. Settlers fled before him, burning and destroying their property as they went. Houston retreated too, keeping his troops just out of reach of Santa Anna and moving ever eastward until he reached the bayou country where the city of Houston now stands. This great retreat was known as the 'Runaway Scrape'.

At the junction of Buffalo Bayou and the San Jacinto River Houston told his little army to get ready for a fight. His short speech contained sixteen words: 'Victory is certain. Trust in God and fear not. And remember the Alamo — Remember the Alamo!'

On the afternoon of 21 April the Mexicans, as was their wont, settled down for their afternoon siesta. Unheard and unseen seven hundred Texans crept through the long grass towards them. The Mexicans awoke to find the enemy upon them. In less than half an hour the battle, one of the most decisive in American history, was over. Santa Anna's army was destroyed and he himself taken prisoner. Texas was 'free'; which meant the Mexicans had lost it.

For ten years after the battle of San Jacinto Texas remained independent. Settlement expanded rapidly. The new republic attracted not only the land-seeking frontier farmers from the neighbouring United States but also a large proportion of adventurers and renegades of all kinds and all nationalities. Drinking, fighting, bragging and carousing

Flag of Texan Republic

became characteristic of the Texans who, by virtue of the fact that they had fought for and won their independence, considered themselves a race apart.

Mexico still refused to recognize Texan independence. There was always the chance that she might send an army across the border. This fear, coupled with the increasing menace from the Indians, turned Austin's original mounted Rangers into an efficient frontier force.

By 1840 the Texas Rangers had their permanent headquarters at San Antonio. They were commanded by Captain John Coffee Hays. In combatting Mexican raids across the border and Indian raids from the west the Rangers learnt to ride hard, fight hard and shoot fast.

The weapons the Texans had brought with them from the east were not all suitable for fighting on horseback. The 'long rifle' or the single-shot duelling pistol did not count for much against hundreds of mounted Indians who could fire a quiverful of arrows from horseback quicker than a Texan could reload.

In 1836, the very year of the Texas revolution, a young American named Samuel Colt patented a revolving pistol. By 1838 'Colt's patent firearms' were being manufactured in New Jersey. But no one was very interested in the gun – no one, that is, until somebody took one of the new Colt 'revolvers' to Texas. Its ability to fire six shots without reloading was just what the Rangers needed, and it is known to have been used by them in 1839.

As the years went by various improvements and modifications were made. The 'six-shooter' became the gun of the west and was an important factor in its final conquest.

Colt revolver

The USA after annexation of Mexican territory

The 'Texas Question' loomed large in United States politics. Many immigrants from the southern states had taken their slaves into Texas with them. Texas, therefore, if admitted to the Union would be a 'slave state'. As such her annexation was violently opposed by the abolitionists.

In 1845 Texans voted overwhelmingly for annexation to the United States and on 29 December Texas was formally admitted to the Union. For the Mexicans, still smouldering and resentful at the humiliation of recent defeats, it was an excuse for a fight. They declared war in 1846. General Zachary Taylor marched towards the Rio Grande accompanied by a company of Texas Rangers.

At the Battle of Buena Vista in February 1847 the Mexicans were utterly defeated and Santa Anna was forced to surrender. By the Treaty of Guadalupe-Hidalgo in 1848 Mexico recognized the United States' title to Texas and Upper California which, in those days, included most of the territory now forming the states of Arizona, California, New Mexico, Utah, Nevada and Colorado.

THE DAYS OF '49

By 1820 California had become a pleasant, if isolated, outpost of the Spanish empire. From about 1790 onwards foreigners began to enter California in increasing numbers. One of these emigrants was John Sutter, a Swiss, who built himself a ranch on the American river in 1840.

Men who visited California never failed to send home glowing reports about the romantic, easy-going province. More and more American eyes turned towards this land of milk and honey which beckoned invitingly from the far side of the treeless plains and the great deserts. By 1846 some seven hundred Americans had settled officially or unofficially, in California.

In that same year John Charles Fremont set out on an expedition in order to explore the Great Basin and the Pacific coast. But the Mexican authorities were convinced that his expedition was part of a design to seize California for the United States. Fremont was ordered out of the country.

He headed towards Oregon but shortly afterwards received a message from Washington which caused him to turn back for California. The American settlers in the old Spanish colony were now convinced that Fremont's intention *was* to seize the area. This theory was reinforced by the arrival of some American naval vessels at Monterey. On 4 June 1846, the settlers 'rebelled' against the Mexicans and proclaimed the 'Bear Flag Republic', so called because the flag they raised bore a star and a grizzly bear.

Colonel Stephen Watts Kearny and a small force of men arrived from New Mexico and within a short time the American flag was flying over California. It must have been one of the easiest conquests in history.

Bear Rebellion flag

With the treaty of Guadalupe-Hidalgo which ended the Mexican war the southern boundary of the USA was finally determined. All the land which forms the present USA was now in her possession. The remaining story of westward expansion is one of filling up and developing the great open spaces that lay between the Mississippi and the California coast.

Settlement of California would no doubt have developed on much the same lines as that of Oregon had it not been for a tremendous discovery at the *hacienda* of John Sutter. The Swiss immigrant had developed his land into an almost entirely self-supporting baronial empire. In 1848 he had begun the construction of a sawmill forty-eight miles above his fort – Sutter's Fort – on the American River, a tributary of the Sacramento. On 24 January 1848, James Marshall, an American carpenter in charge of operations, was inspecting a newly-dug ditch when he noticed some flecks of bright metal. He took a sample of his find to Sutter. Tests confirmed that the substance was gold. Sutter tried to keep the discovery a secret but too many workmen were involved and the news leaked out.

The whispered rumour of 'Gold on the Sacramento!' grew into a mighty roar which was soon to reverberate from California to the rest of America and thence to the world.

All over California men flocked to the 'diggings'. In the little town of San Francisco business houses closed, churches emptied, sailors deserted their ships, blacksmiths, tailors, shopkeepers, school teachers, all left their work, humped picks and shovels on their backs and set out for Sutter's Mill. In January 1848 there were more than 2,000 men living in San Francisco. By February all but five of them had left for the gold fields.

News of the discovery did not reach the eastern states until November 1848 when the military governor of California, Colonel R. B. Mason, sent an official report to Washington accompanied by a tea caddy full of gold dust valued at $3,910.10.

The eastern press took up the story and the rush was on. Thousands were lured from their homes to try their luck in golden California.

The problem was how to get to the promised land. Some thought the easiest route would be by sea; all the way round Cape Horn and up the Pacific coast. Throughout the Eastern states posters appeared advertising ships about to sail for California. From the North American ports round the Cape to California was 17,000 miles.

San Francisco in November 1848

Californian clipper

For most passengers a trip round the Cape meant 130 days of hell, in overcrowded, unseaworthy vessels, with bad food and terrible storms. There was no chance of a return trip for on arrival at San Francisco the crews deserted and went to try their luck at the diggings.

Both sailing ships and paddle steamers made this long and often perilous journey. But the finest ships to round the Cape, specially built for speed, ability to work in light winds and cross belts of calm, were sailing ships – the Californian Clippers. Tall masts, sharp hulls and wide spread of sail sent these beautiful birds of the ocean skimming across the foam at a spanking rate. The famous *Flying Cloud* made the run from New York in nearly half the average sailing time.

Companies were formed specially to buy ships to make the sea passage and to share all profits from gold mining. But once the gold fields were reached it was every man's gains for himself and the Company was forgotten.

The scandalously high prices charged by the shipping companies for the dangerous sea passage to California compelled the majority of would-be miners to face the trials and tribulations of the cheaper overland trip. Now it was that the ex-fur-traders and mountain men came into their own. The trails they had blazed and the knowledge they had gained proved invaluable to the forty-niners who gathered on the banks of the Missouri at Westport or Independence in preparation for their two-thousand mile journey.

At these 'jumping-off places' the forty-niners bought their wagons and oxen and stocked up with food and supplies. The majority joined wagon trains commanded by 'wagon masters' (usually one-time mountain men). The forty-niners were pitifully ignorant of the hardships they had to face. Many loaded almost the whole contents of their homes into their wagons or bought cheap vehicles and indifferent animals which could never survive the journey. Conscientious captains inspected the trains before they started and advised the travellers not to load the wagons too heavily. Many would not heed the advice and in consequence, as the going got harder, the California trail became littered with broken-down wagons, discarded clothing and pieces of furniture including chests of drawers and double beds.

The California trail

The most generally used trail followed the Kansas River to Fort Kearney and then the old fur trader's route along the North Platte River to South Pass. Here the trail divided. Some emigrants turned south and followed the Mormon trail to Salt Lake City where they found welcome help in the way of food and supplies. Others stayed further north heading for Soda Springs and Fort Hall and thence south-westward across the Humboldt Valley to where the two routes again merged at City of Rocks. Then came the crossing of the dreaded Humboldt Desert or 'Sink' and the final climb over the lofty Sierra Nevada mountains into California.

Because the Sierra Nevada had to be crossed when they were free of snow the emigrants could not leave Independence earlier than April or later than May. Parties leaving after May would find themselves trapped in the mountains as happened to the ill-fated Donner party who got lost in the snow in 1846 and resorted to cannibalism in order to survive. In April and May 1849 the white-topped wagons streamed endlessly out of Independence and Westport. Some 50,000 men, women and children are reckoned to have gone over-land that season.

Emigrant camp

Wagon master

The lines of wagons rolled slowly across the plains. Sometimes men and animals were blinded and parched by the heat and dust; sometimes the camps were washed out by torrential rains which turned the ground into a quagmire in which the wagons stuck fast. But even so the first part of the journey was a picnic compared with what was to follow. At night there was singing and dancing around the camp fires and the discomforts of the journey were forgotten.

The wagoners were soon brought face to face with reality. Broken-down wagons, horses and oxen dying of thirst, families proceeding on foot carrying what possessions they could manage on their backs, precious articles abandoned at the side of the trail, men digging graves, were the portents of the tough going ahead. Yet there could be no turning back. To be sure of reaching California safely an average of seventeen miles a day was essential.

By the time the Rocky Mountains were reached the weakest and less well-equipped had already fallen by the wayside. The long climb up to the summit of the Continental Divide was strenuous but the air was fresh and cool after the hot dusty plains. The great pass discovered by the fur traders was some thirty miles wide. Those who reached it took fresh heart; they were now half-way towards their goal.

For many miles the trail followed the Humboldt River
through a series of valleys and ravines. Sometimes the river
bed was almost dry. Sometimes it was merely a series of pools,
all strongly alkaline and undrinkable. At the Humboldt Sink
the river disappeared altogether, sucked up by the hot
white sand. From that point to the Carson River, a distance
of forty miles, there was not a drop of water anywhere along
the trail.

In preparation for crossing the Sink all available receptacles
were filled with water. Every wagon wheel was soaked in it;
tongues, axles and brakes were checked; animals were
watered and fed. The white ashy dust rose in stifling
billows around the line of wagons as they plunged into the
desert. The oxen sank belly-deep into the alkali dust.
Wagons had to be man-handled over some of the worst
places. The alkali stung the eyes and burnt the lungs and
throat. Half-blinded, scorched by the burning sun, nauseated
by the stench of the thousands of dead cattle and mules that
lined the route, the forty-niners plodded on. Those still in
possession of their wagons were haunted by the sight and
sound of the less fortunate whose transport had failed and
who stood hopelessly and desperately amongst their belongings begging for a lift.

The grave markers grew more frequent as dysentery and,
worst of all, cholera took their toll. Men and women went
mad; animals stampeded as they caught the smell of the
river from afar, overturning camps and wagons in their
crazy rush to reach the water. In fifteen miles one chronicler
counted 350 dead horses, 280 oxen and 120 mules. One
thousand wagons had been totally abandoned.

Bound for the
Promised Land

Those who survived the terrible crossing found relief in the water and shady cottonwood trees of the Carson River. Here groups of anxious men and women waited for news of lost friends or relatives; relief camps were set up to tend to the sick. Unscrupulous traders arrived from California with food and supplies which they sold at exorbitant prices to the weary travellers. Gamblers, too, pitched their tents to welcome the unsuspecting and many a forty-niner lost his last few belongings at their hands.

Rested and refreshed, the survivors set off to tackle the last big hurdle – the crossing of the Sierra Nevada. It was a task to daunt the fittest men, let alone the weary, ill-fed, suffering forty-niners, weak from dysentery and other diseases. Unlike the ascent to South Pass which is very gradual, the passes through the Sierra Nevada are some of the steepest in the world. At the summit the miners found themselves higher than the highest pass of the Italian Alps. It took ten mules pulling and ten more men pushing from behind to get the wagons up and over the last two miles.

Sometimes the way was too steep for this method. Trees were then cut down and block and tackle improvised to

haul the wagons up the slopes. Heavily ballasted wagons let down the slope acted as a counter weight to help other wagons up. Sometimes the concerted efforts of all available men and mules were organized to haul the wagons up one at a time. Sometimes the ropes broke under the strain and the wagon and belongings of an entire family went crashing down to their destruction. Occasionally part of the family went too. The danger was not over even when the slopes were climbed; the roads and trails through the mountains were perilous and barely wide enough to take a wagon. A stumble, a slip or the sudden fright of a mule or ox team was enough to send a wagon crashing to the rocks below.

From the mountain streams came a dreadful stench, evidence that the climb had taken its toll of many animals almost within sight of their goal. Those humans who toiled up the steep sides were kept going only by the thought of the fortunes ahead. At the summit there was a natural break in the rock wall, forming a kind of gateway. Through this gap they saw the promised land lying before them. Their cares were forgotten as they tumbled down the mountainside towards the golden state.

Placer mining involved no excavating; gold was panned out of the river beds

At the end of the trail was Hangtown – later to be called by the more genteel name of Placerville. This collection of tents and shacks was the immigrant's first experience of a mining community. Most of those who had survived the gruelling journey and thought their troubles were now over were to be sadly disillusioned. Saloons and gambling dens abounded. Prices of food and mining equipment soared.

In the early days of the rush many miners had indeed panned out fortunes and the occasional nugget worth several thousand dollars was still to be found. For the great majority of forty-niners, however, mining consisted of laboriously washing the gravel from the river beds, a process which involved physical labour of the hardest kind. Few of those who arrived exhausted by the wagon journey were able to survive many days of standing, often waist deep, in the icy cold river while the sun blazed fiercely down from above.

This new frontier was unlike any that had gone before. Up to now frontier communities had consisted mainly of *families* who wished to make a home and living out of the land they settled on. The gold rush, by its very nature, attracted the speculators, the opportunists, the adventurers and the gamblers. No one bothered to build proper houses or grow food; they were too busy trying to wash out the elusive gold dust.

Not only Americans but foreigners from all over the world were infected with the gold fever. In England shipping companies announced the departure of many vessels 'From London to California direct'; in France lotteries called 'The Lotteries of the Golden Ingot' offered trips to the gold-fields as prizes. The Chinese who arrived in great numbers on the Pacific coast opened laundries and restaurants and laid the foundation of today's Chinese quarter of San Francisco. Shop-keepers, builders, estate agents, bankers, prospered as San Francisco grew from a cluster of tents and shacks into a flourishing town.

Criminals and renegades of all kinds went to California to escape justice and seek their fortunes. In the rough and tumble of the mining camps riotous living, thieving, brawling

Chinese immigrant

and murder were rife. To protect their lives and property settlements formed 'vigilante' committees which took upon themselves the task of enforcing law and order. Their system of justice was rough. Trials were hasty or non-existent. Men were sentenced and hanged at the demand of the mob. The tough mining communities of California thus set a pattern of frontier justice which was to become a characteristic of the rip-roaring cow towns of the 1860s and '70s.

The gold rush made a few men rich. It ruined many more

and took the lives of one in every five. Prospectors wandered from place to place hoping for a lucky strike. Some stayed in California until the discovery of gold in Colorado, Nevada, Montana and the Yukon later in the century lured them to fresh fields. Others gave up gold mining and turned to farming. They were, perhaps, the wisest for, as time went by, it gradually became clear that California's future lay in her golden grain and sunshine rather than in the metal from her hills. The gold rush petered out, the mining towns fell into ruins. Only a handful of prospectors still searched patiently in the hills. The 'lone prospector' entered America's folklore.

The results of the gold rush were far reaching. Apart from the growth and prosperity of such towns as San Francisco and Sacramento, the Mormon community at Salt Lake City benefited enormously from the constant stream of travellers with whom the Saints carried on a prosperous trade. As California grew and developed so did the need for faster communication between west and east. This, as we shall

see, was a major factor in the development of those lands which still remained bare of white settlement: the area, that is, between the Missouri and the Sierra Nevada.

The early pioneers considered these treeless plains and barren plateaux merely as a barrier to their progress to more inviting lands; a barrier to be crossed as quickly as possible. Not until the railway had joined California to the eastern states did anyone except the Mormons think of trying to make a home in this unpromising region.

French voyageur passing a keelboat

THE WAY WEST

The first trailmakers in America were the buffalo. Indians followed the animals' trails from earliest times. Both Indians and white men used the rivers as a means of transport. In the north the birch-bark canoes of the Indians were adopted by all hunters. As the demand for bigger vessels grew traders built 'flatboats' which were huge rafts of roughly joined timbers.

The laden 'flats' were floated down the river to New Orleans. They were unable to make headway against the current so, when they reached port, instead of returning they were broken up and sold for lumber. Flatboats gave way to keelboats.

Keelboats were great barges made manoeuvrable by wooden keels and propelled and steered by huge wooden 'sweeps' or oars. Keelboats could make the journey back upstream but only by means of enormous human exertion. The crew had to pole, paddle or pull the boats along. Towing was by means of a rope or 'cordelle'. 'Cordellers' waded through the shallow water at the edge of the river towing their craft behind them.

Keelboatmen became legendary characters. Their brags, coarse jests and courage have been immortalized in the folk stories of Mike Fink and other rip-roaring 'half-men, half-alligators' as keelboatmen described themselves. They were the toughest and most feared men on the river.

But their day was short-lived. On 11 October 1811, the

An early steamboat

steamboat *New Orleans*, the first on any western river, left Pittsburgh. In January 1812, she arrived in New Orleans; the great age of steamboating had begun.

The first steamboat to successfully navigate the Mississippi (and the Ohio) *upstream* was the *Enterprise*. This remarkable feat was achieved as early as 1815 – the year of Waterloo.

Flatboats and keelboats continued to take their cargoes downstream for some years but by the 1830s steam held a virtual monopoly of all freight and passenger traffic on the Mississippi and its main tributaries.

Soon steam boats were plying the Mississippi, the Missouri,

the Ohio and even lesser western waterways as well; anywhere, in fact, where there was enough water to float them. Pittsburgh, Louisville and St Louis grew into bustling inland ports.

By 1829 more than two hundred steamboats were plying western rivers. Technical improvements resulted in faster journeys and cheaper freight rates. In 1815 the *Enterprise* took twenty-five days and two hours to cover the 1,350 miles from New Orleans to Louisville. In 1853 the *Eclipse* made the same journey in four days and nine hours.

The rapidity with which the west was settled coincides with the introduction of the steamboat. Western population in 1815 was estimated to be about one million persons; by 1850 it was six million and twenty years later fifteen million. The prosperity of the west was reflected in the style of the steamboat and the luxury of river travel. Tourists, business-men, planters, gamblers and other adventurers travelled in glittering upper-class accommodation. The white paint and the gilt 'gingerbread' carving of the woodwork earned them the name of 'floating palaces'. State rooms were equal to the best rooms found in hotels along the shore – even in the bigger towns. The dining rooms, bars, ballrooms and gambling saloons were the last word in luxury. The best orchestras and entertainers were engaged to keep the passengers amused. Every boat carried its professional gamblers; sometimes they were on the pay roll of the steamboat company who took a percentage of all winnings.

The lower class or 'deck passengers' – usually emigrants – travelled on the bottom deck along with the livestock, cotton bales and other river freight.

The big Mississippi boats usually had two paddle wheels, one on each side. On other shallower western rivers smaller single-wheeled boats, known as 'sternwheelers', were used. If one of these small flat-bottomed craft ran into a sandbar – a frequent occurence on the muddy western rivers – it merely reversed and used its big wooden stern wheel to dig its way back into deeper water.

The great age of steamboats was just before the Civil War. By 1880 they were on the decline and were soon superseded by the railroads.

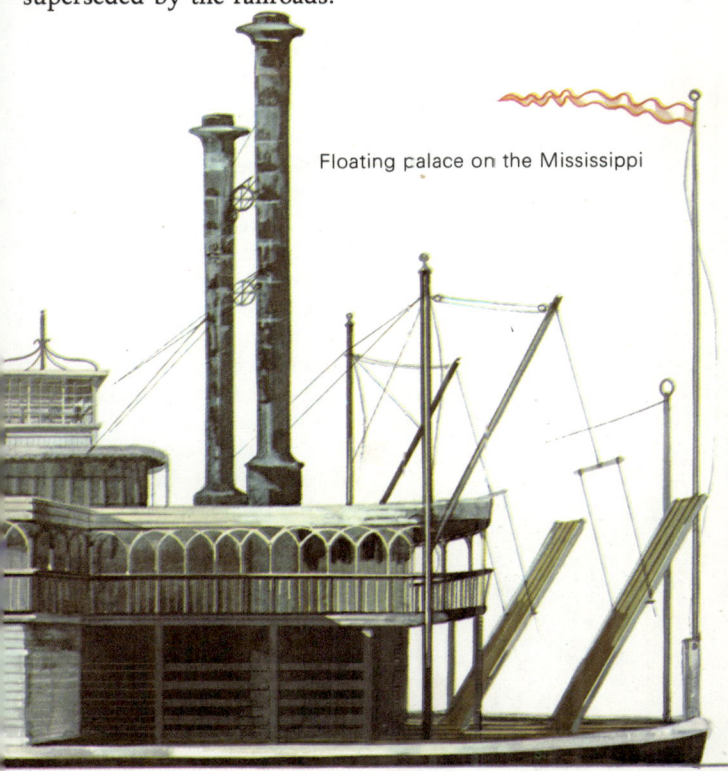

Floating palace on the Mississippi

The Erie Canal

As most early settlements were along the shores of the Mississippi and its tributaries, nearly all river commerce tended southward to New Orleans. In northern Ohio, Indiana, Michigan and other places not actually situated on a tributary of the Mississippi, farmers experienced great difficulty in getting their produce to market. For some time there had been talk of providing an outlet by means of a canal which would connect the Great Lakes in the west with the Hudson River in the east.

Work on this project began in 1817. By 1825 the Erie Canal, five hundred miles of man-made waterway, connected Buffalo with New York. The canal was a great national and financial success. Other towns in the east such as Boston, Philadelphia and Baltimore began to build canals of their own. The state of Pennsylvania built a whole system of waterways connecting Philadelphia to Pittsburgh. In 1832 the Ohio Canal was opened. It joined the Ohio River with Lake Erie and enabled Ohio farmers to ship their flour and wheat all the way to New York by water.

Canals became a favourite

means of transport for emigrants to the north-west. They also served to open up the great timber industry in the heavily wooded areas of Michigan.

In 1806 the vociferous demands of western farmers for better communications with their markets led Thomas Jefferson to sign the Cumberland Road Bill. By 1812 this great highway, one of the finest in America's history, stretched 130 miles beyond Cumberland Gap. The first regular freight and passenger wagons rolled over its surface.

The characteristic 'covered wagon' originated in the eighteenth century among the Dutch settlers in the Conestoga Valley of Pennsylvania. It was a sturdy, rather clumsy vehicle. Its front wheels were two feet smaller in diameter than the rear ones. The white canvas top on a framework of sturdy ribs gave protection from the weather. Its boat-like appearance earned it the nickname of 'prairie schooner'.

Conestoga wagons were used extensively in the Santa Fe trade and by the emigrants to Oregon and California. Freight companies also used them in preference to pack trains as they gave stronger defence against Indian attacks.

A Conestoga wagon

61

As communities and towns became established, westerners soon felt the need for a more comfortable means of passenger transportation and a faster mail service. Both were supplied by the stage coach. By 1820 stage coach lines were already carrying mail and passengers between St Louis and the east.

The most famous stage coach developed in America was the Concord. It was named after the town in New Hampshire where it was made by the firm of Abbot and Downing. Its graceful, egg-shaped body swinging on leather 'thorough-braces', between the axles, offered a fast and comfortable journey.

Although at the time of the California gold rush stage coach lines were operating as far as Santa Fe and Salt Lake City there was no regular transcontinental service. Even within the state of California itself transportation was most inadequate, supplies for the gold fields being carried mainly on mule trains. Soon, however, enterprising newcomers to the golden state realized that they would grow richer transporting passengers and goods than by gold mining.

Regular stage lines gradually became established between the larger towns of California.

The miner's hunger for news and goods from 'back east' gave rise to a peculiarly American enterprise – the Express Company. The term 'express' meant the transportation of letters and other commodities by special messenger.

In 1841 Henry Wells, a steamboat operator, founded an express company to operate between Albany and Buffalo in the state of New York. The company carried letters at a cheaper rate than the post office. In 1843 William George Fargo went to work for Wells as a messenger. A year later Wells invited Fargo to become his partner in the formation of an express company to serve Chicago, Cincinnati and St Louis. By 1852 Wells and Fargo were strong enough to challenge the powerful Adams Express Company already operating in California.

The first sixty-five packages to be handled by Wells Fargo's California office arrived at San Francisco on 11 July 1852, the messengers having made the perilous journey by land and sea via the Isthmus of Panama. From San Francisco the packets were delivered to the addressees.

In 1855, following a financial crisis in California, many banks, including that of Adams and Company, failed. Wells Fargo, however, being financed from the east, weathered the storm. At the end of the crisis they emerged triumphantly as the greatest express-banking business in California.

Although Wells Fargo had secured a monopoly of the express business in California it had, as yet, no stage line. The first mail and passenger service between St Louis and San Francisco was the Butterfield Overland Mail. A rail service was available as far as Tipton, Missouri but from thereon the only fast travel was by stage. Altogether 139 stage stations were set up along the trail. It ran from Tipton to Fort Smith, Arkansas, through Indian territory to the Red River in Texas, south-west across that state, west across southern New Mexico to Fort Yuma, California and from there to San Francisco. This wide sweep to the south was thought necessary to avoid the mountain snows.

The first stage left Tipton junction on 16 September 1858 and reached San Francisco, after a journey of almost 2,758 miles, on Sunday, 10 October. By 1860 Butterfield was handling more mail than the Pacific steamers and was operating twice weekly.

The Butterfield stage route was the longest on record. More than 800 men were needed to operate the line. Most stages ran day and night, with changes of horse teams every

ten or twenty miles. Passengers could try to sleep on the stages or stop overnight at the relay stations.

The man responsible for the safety and comfort of the passengers and of the mail was the stage driver who became a highly revered character. His word was law. The seat next to him on the driving box was the most coveted. It was allocated by him to the most important passenger unless, as was often the case, it was occupied by a shot-gun guard. Stage drivers were expert in handling their teams of highly spirited horses which they drove at a hard gallop over the most difficult terrain.

Drivers were venerated by everyone. Most of them had nicknames such as 'Buffalo Jim', 'Curly Dan', or 'One-eyed Charlie'. Hank Monk, perhaps the most celebrated stage driver of all, became the legendary figure of the plains just as Davy Crockett had become the hero of the backwoods and Mike Fink the terror of the Mississippi.

Hank Monk, a famous stage coach driver

Another famous freighting and staging concern of the plains was that of Russell, Majors and Waddell. They operated freight wagons along the central route between Missouri and Sacramento. In 1860 they brought into operation a new and romantic method of fast communication – the Pony Express. Pony Express messengers were boys, chosen for their lightness, horsemanship and physical endurance. Speed was all important. Special lightweight saddles and stirrups and a specially designed mail bag known as a 'mochila' were devised. The mochila is best described as a leather blanket with four pockets. It fitted over the saddle by means of two holes through which the saddle horn and cantle protruded. The mail was carried in the oilskin-lined pockets. At each relay station the rider dismounted, threw the mochila onto a fresh pony, swung himself on the top of it and continued on his way.

The new service undertook to deliver letters from east to west in thirteen days. The speed for the 1,966 miles covered by a Pony Expressman had to average nine miles an hour come blizzards, rainstorms, scorching heat or hold-ups. The record time for the trip was for the delivery of Lincoln's

Pony Express rider

Denver city

inaugural address in March 1861. It took seven days and seventeen hours.

But in spite of its great achievements the Pony Express lasted only eighteen months. Ever since its inauguration the telegraph lines had been slowly extending across the plains. The Pacific Telegraph Company were building eastward from Virginia City and westward from Omaha. On 24 October 1861, the two parties of workmen met and the transcontinental telegraph was completed. The next day the Sacramento Union announced the discontinuance of the Pony Express.

There still remained, however, a demand for a quick postal and passenger route between the east and west, a demand which was intensified from 1859 onwards when gold was discovered in the Pike's Peak area of Colorado.

Once again the covered wagons rolled westward and, indeed, eastward as disappointed Californian miners decided to try their luck at the new diggings. Once again the speculators and promoters cashed in on the credulity of the emigrants and promised them untold riches in the new Eldorado; and once again most prospectors were doomed to disappointment. Wagons which, on their way out, carried the cheerful slogan 'Pike's Peak or Bust!' retraced their tracks bearing the mournful words 'Busted by God!'

In February, 1860 the Central Overland California and Pike's Peak Express Company came into operation. In 1861 the Central Overland ran into financial difficulties and was bought out by Ben Holladay, an energetic ruthless westerner. In 1866 Wells Fargo offered to buy out Holladay's Overland. At first Holladay refused. But already the railroad which was to put an end to stage coaching altogether was creeping across his territory. Holladay reckoned it was better to sell out rather than see his empire crumble. So on 1 November 1866. Wells Fargo purchased the entire Holladay system and thus gained control of almost every stage and express service in the west.

Wells Fargo became a national institution. Every western town had its Wells Fargo office. Every kind of object from gold dust to children was entrusted to its care. By 1868 Wells Fargo were running passenger trips from New York to California in only thirteen days.

As more and more valuables were carried road agents became an increasing menace. Soon almost all stage coaches carried shot-gun guards and an ever increasing number of detectives were employed by the Company. Between them they kept the road agents at bay. Between 1875 and 1883 there were 206 convictions for robbery, 11 road agents were killed while resisting arrest and 7 officially hanged.

As the railroads spread so stage coaching died. But the express and banking interests of Wells Fargo lived on into the railway age. Its messengers continued to carry express material from one end of the continent to the other using the iron horse as their means of transport.

THE GREAT AMERICAN RAILROAD

In the east the canals and steamboats hardly had time to develop to their full capacity before they had to face competition from a much faster and more flexible means of transportation – the railways. Thirteen miles of railway track were already in use in 1830 but it was not until 1831 that steam power was introduced.

By 1840 there were nearly 5,000 miles of steam railroad in operation. The railroad was well on its way to becoming the principal means of transport but its progress struck a number of snags. A total of $250,000,000 had been invested in canals. The investors could hardly be expected to welcome a means of transport faster and cheaper than their own.

'Canals', said one canal owner, 'are God's own highway, operating on the soft bosom of the fluid that comes straight from heaven. The railroad stems direct from Hell.'

But, in spite of fierce opposition, by 1860 the Erie Railroad Company had supplanted the Erie Canal as the main link between New York and the western wheat and meat-producing states, and the whole of the United States east of the Mississippi was criss-crossed with railway lines.

In 1856 the Rock Island Railway built a bridge across the

MOTHERS LOOK OUT FOR YOUR CHILDREN!
ARTISANS, MECHANICS, CITIZENS!
DREADFUL CASUALITY!
LOCOMOTIVE RAIL ROAD!
SUBURB OF NEW YORK!!
RALLY PEOPLE in the Majesty of your Strength and forbid
OUTRAGE!

Poster attacking railroads

Mississippi from Rock Island, Illinois on the eastern bank to Davenport, Iowa, on the western side.

Two weeks after the first locomotive had crossed the Mississippi a boat called the *Effie Afton*, property of the New Orleans and Louisville Packet Company, collided with the bridge and caught fire. The owners of the *Effie Afton* sued the Rock Island Railroad for damages, claiming that the bridge was an obstruction to river traffic.

The railroad company, realizing that the future of railroads in the west depended on the outcome of the case, hired Abraham Lincoln, then virtually an unknown lawyer, to defend them.

Lincoln did not actually accuse anyone of deliberately wrecking railway property but his speech convinced the jury that the bridge presented no material obstruction had the boat been managed with 'reasonable care and skill'.

Lincoln was one of the few men of the time to realize the potentialities of the railroad. He foresaw how it could bring prosperity and development to the vast lands beyond the Mississippi. The Rock Island bridge stayed and the railroad was ready to begin its westward advance.

71

Asa Whitney held meetings all over the country

But for several years the Mississippi remained the eastern limit of the railroads. In the comparatively well-populated eastern states, where railways were built to connect community to community, the companies were assured of passengers and freight. West of the Mississippi, however, promoters saw only mile after mile of sparsely inhabited prairie or mountains.

Nevertheless far-sighted men continued to press for a railway to span the continent. One of the most persistent was Asa Whitney. As early as 1844 he proposed to Congress a plan for a transcontinental railroad from Lake Michigan to the Pacific. Whitney held meetings all over the country, pointing out the advantages of a quick route to the Orient and other benefits of the proposed line.

Whitney came up against powerful opposition from ship builders, clipper owners and stage coach companies. His plan came to nothing but it was due to his fervour and enthusiasm that the idea of a transcontinental railroad became implanted in the public mind.

In 1854 Theodore Dehone Judah, a railway engineer from Connecticut, was engaged as chief engineer for a projected Californian railroad to run from Sacramento to the placer mining district in the Sierra foothills. Having completed the line to the gold diggings, he was asked to survey a wagon road to connect California with the expanding silver towns of Nevada. Judah made the survey but not for a wagon road. His report showed a practical route for a railway through the mountains and on across the plains to the Atlantic.

In 1859 Judah staged a Pacific Railroad Convention in San Francisco. Later he was sent to Washington to lay his plan before Congress. By now politicians were more disposed to listen than they had been in Asa Whitney's day. The year was 1862 and the Civil War was in progress. Above all Abraham Lincoln, always a champion of the railroad, had become President.

Lincoln was convinced that an important factor in preserving the Union was to establish fast communication between east and west. California was of particular interest as it was feared she might join the Confederacy. Lincoln considered that the building of a transcontinental railroad would prevent California's secession.

The problem of financing such a project seemed insuperable. Lincoln's one asset was the government-owned land which stretched west of the Missouri to the Californian border. He decided that huge grants of this potentially valuable property should be allotted to anybody who would undertake the building of a railroad to the Pacific.

On 1 July 1862, the Pacific Railroad Act was passed by Congress. It appointed two companies to build and operate it. One was the Union Pacific which was to build westward from the 100th meridian in the territory of Nebraska to the California line; the other, the Central Pacific, was to build eastward from Sacramento.

The act allotted to each company a four-hundred-foot right of way for the actual construction of the railroad together with alternate square-mile sections of public lands on both sides of the track. The project, therefore, became a race between the two companies to lay most track and thereby obtain the greater proportion of land grants.

The men who financed and directed the Central Pacific consisted of Leland Stanford, Charles Crocker, Mark Hopkins and Collis P. Huntington. They became known as 'the Big

Four'. Their sole object in railroad building was to make money. They had none of Theodore Judah's vision or integrity.

The first shovelful of earth was turned at Sacramento on 8 January 1863. The Big Four's object was to lay the first forty miles of track as quickly as possible and qualify for the government bonds. Judah thought that besides being built quickly the line should be built *well*. He abhorred the cheap and shoddy proposals of the Big Four. A break was inevitable. Judah was bought out for 100,000 dollars. He sailed for New York where he hoped to raise enough money to buy out the Big Four but he caught yellow fever and died. Thus it was the Big Four who received the great profits and the glory that were the rewards of constructing the Central Pacific.

Judah had already surveyed the Central Pacific's route as far as the western slopes of the Sierras. The first part of the Central Pacific's operation was, therefore, comparatively easy. It was when they found themselves in the uncharted high Sierras that the company's troubles really began.

Routes of Union Pacific and Central Pacific

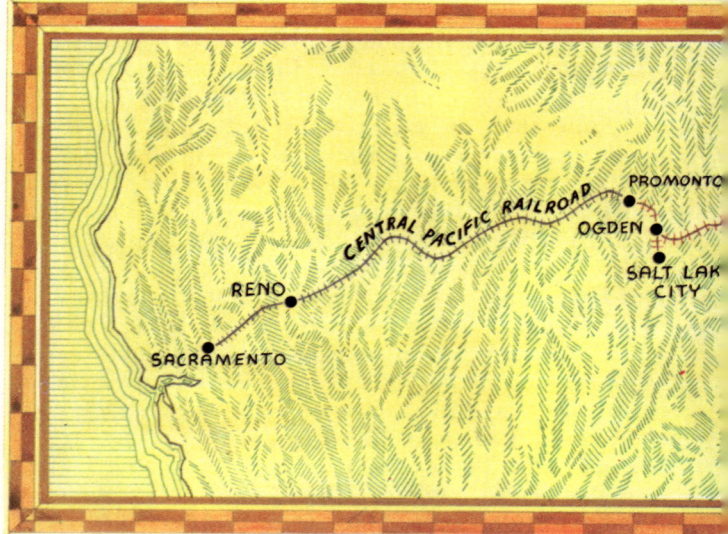

Building the Central Pacific Railroad

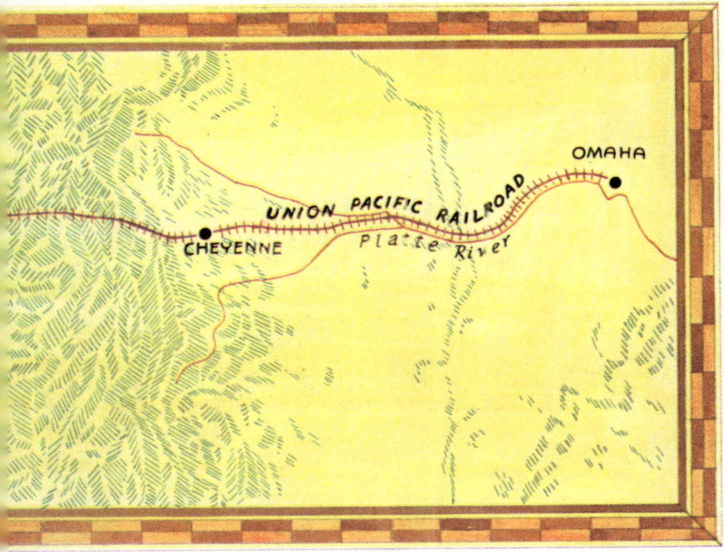

Charles Crocker, who was in charge of grading and track laying, could not find anything like enough labourers to carry the railroad through the Sierras. Those he did scrape together would, after only a few days work, disappear in the direction of the 'diggings' taking the Company's tools with them.

Crocker had a Chinese manservant called Ah Ling. He suggested that Crocker should try Chinese labour. Many Chinese had been attracted to California and were working principally as laundrymen, caterers or servants. Crocker hired fifty Chinese as an experiment. The tall tough American graders considered the tiny pig-tailed Chinese a huge joke.

On the first day of their employment the Chinese set up a neat and efficient camp at end of the track, cooked themselves a meal of rice then bedded down for the night. At sun-up they were hard at work hewing, blasting and digging their way into the mountains. They worked so hard that within twelve hours Crocker wired to Sacramento for a further supply of Chinese workers. Within six months more than 2,000 had been specially shipped over from China. Their demands were few. They saved up their wages and caused little trouble. Crocker grew very fond of them.

Chinese labour on the railroads (*below* and *right*)

They became known as 'Crocker's pets'.

The sheer, granite rock-face of the Sierra Nevada would have presented a formidable problem for modern construction engineers equipped with bulldozers, mechanical shovels and dynamite. Crocker's pets worked only with picks, shovels, saws and charges of black powder. Black powder had to be fired from close up and was liable to blow up the igniter if he didn't run away fast enough. Trees had to be cut down. Loads of precious earth were hauled by donkeys to fill up the canyons and level out the grade. Deep canyons were spanned by trestle bridges.

When the first bitter winter closed in, heavy falls of snow stopped all construction work except in one tunnel. A few valiant Chinese hacked away in the bowels of the mountain all through the winter and did not see daylight again until they emerged at the far end of the tunnel the following spring. The warm weather brought a new danger; avalanches swept away bridges, track and men.

Crocker had learned a hard lesson and was determined

Union Pacific gets under way

not to be caught napping the following winter. Throughout the summer his lumber-jacks cut down thousands of trees from which the engineers built long wooden snowsheds to act as a roof over the railroad. By spring 1869, forty miles of sheds had been built. Under the sheds' protection the Chinese were able to keep on working right through the following winter. The sheds also kept the track free from snow and open to the trains. The sheds were not abandoned until snow ploughs and other snow-fighting equipment made them obsolete.

The engineer in charge of construction of the Union Pacific line was General Dodge who, because of the war, could not take up his appointment at once.

The Union Pacific had not the advantage of a ready-made survey such as Theodore Judah had handed to the Central. Before any construction work could begin surveying parties had to be sent deep into the vast, uninhabited plains area between the Mississippi and the Rockies to map out a route. The further west the surveyors went the fiercer became the Indians. However buffalo proved the worse nuisance. The animals would use the surveyor's wooden markers as scratching posts and knock them down. Surveyors were constantly having to retrace their steps and set the markers up again.

Sioux war parties were very active round the Laramie mountains through which surveyors were having great trouble in finding a route. An army contingent was sent into the area to quell the unrest. One of its commanders was General Dodge. His scout was mountain man Jim Bridger. One day as a patrol was returning to Fort Laramie, Bridger reported that a party of Indians was lying in wait along the trail. He advised Dodge to skirt around the hills at full speed if he was to avoid the ambush. Dodge gave the order to skirt the hills but, to Bridger's dismay, instead of heading directly for the fort, the general took out his notebook and began to mark the courses of the creeks and rivers and the rise and fall in land level.

At last, with the Indians hot on their heels, Bridger led the troops to the safety of the fort. The soldiers were thankful to Bridger for saving their scalps. To General Dodge

General Dodge and Jim Bridger in the mountains

Irish 'Tarrier'

the exploit meant only one thing – he had discovered a practicable route through the mountains for the Union Pacific.

When General Dodge finally took up his appointment as chief engineer the Union Pacific really got under way. Surveyors and graders pressed ahead. General Jack Casement was construction engineer. The men he employed were ex-soldiers or newly-arrived immigrants from Ireland. They were a tough rough lot. The Irish, it was said, dug their way across the Great Plains like 'dogs digging for bones'. They became known as 'Tarriers' which was the way the Irish pronounced 'terriers'.

Casement organized track laying as though it were a military operation. The exact number of rails and spikes needed for a particular section were brought to 'end of track' in trucks. They were unloaded by twelve men who on the command 'Up! Forward!' raised and carried each rail to its position. On the command 'Ready! Down!' the rail was lowered onto the ties. Other workers followed behind driving in the spikes, tamping down the earth and bolting the rails together. At the end of 1866 the Union Pacific had laid only forty miles of rails; by the end of 1867 'end of track' was 550 miles west of Omaha.

As well as the actual labour of laying the track and the arduous job of hauling every stick of timber across the treeless plains, the workers on the Union Pacific faced constant attack from Indians. They could expect to drop their picks and shovels and take up their rifles to defend themselves at any time.

In the wake of the railroad builders came an army of gamblers, thieves and prostitutes. At 'end of track', alongside the company's bunkhouses, cookhouses and supply depots a miniature town of saloons and 'hotels' would spring up. A new 'end of track' town developed every fifty miles, the rough element moving westward with the railroad.

Many famous western towns grew up in this way. Cheyenne, in Wyoming for example, where the railroad supply camp was located all one winter. More often, though, these 'hells on wheels' as the railroad boom towns were called, became extinct as the line moved westward.

Saloon Keeper

81

Spring of 1868. The Central Pacific had conquered the mountains and were moving out on to the rolling plains of Nevada. The competition between the two companies became acute. In March 1869, the Tarriers announced that they had laid a record figure of six miles of track in a single day. In April 'Crocker's Pets' replied by laying ten miles. The press back east printed track laying figures with all the excitement of a horse race. Both companies strove their utmost to out-lay the other. They were so taken up by their efforts that for some time they failed to see that the courses of the two tracks had overlapped and were running parallel to each other! The Irish realized it first. They saw the Chinese working up on the higher ground. The Irish didn't like the look of them. Somebody fired a shot. The Chinese, who weren't armed, rolled big boulders down on to the Union Pacific track. The Irish retaliated by blowing up a Chinese crew with a charge of black powder.

The officials of both railroad companies and representatives of the government met in Washington to decide on a meeting

The last spike is driven home on 10 May 1869

point before the track layers started a minor war. Congress ordered the two railroads to make a junction at a shack town called Promontory in Utah territory.

10 May 1869, was the day on which the rails were to be officially joined. From the west came the Central Pacific's wood-burning locomotive *Jupiter*, decorated in red and gold and pulling a train of gaudily painted carriages. From the east came the Union Pacific's coal-burning green and gold locomotive number 119. Bands played. The two locomotives moved slowly up to end of track and came to a stop facing each other. The final tie made of Californian laurel was placed in position. The Central Pacific's President Stanford drove home a golden spike with a silver sledge hammer.

When the last spike had been driven home the two engines inched forward until their pilots touched. A telegraphist tapped out the news to the world:

'The last rail is laid
The last spike is driven
The Pacific Railroad is finished.'

With the completion of the Union Pacific, financing railways became a mania. States granted charters. The Federal Government granted public lands. Speculation and corruption were rife; lines were built that ended in nowhere; in the scramble for state bonds and government subsidies fortunes were made and lost.

The second transcontinental line, the Northern Pacific, although chartered in 1864, did not complete its enormous struggle against terrain, climate and bankruptcy until 1883 when it finally linked Lake Superior with Puget Sound. By 1893 James J. Hill had completed his privately constructed Great Northern railroad (without federal subsidy) to Seattle.

Further south, companies large and small struggled and fought their way across the plains and mountains. The Kansas Pacific reached Abilene in 1866. It was while working for this company that William Frederick Cody earned his famous sobriquet of Buffalo Bill. He was hired by a railroad contractor to keep the railroad construction camps in meat. For seventeen months Cody worked on the job and personally slaughtered 4,280 buffalo.

The Atchison, Topeka and Santa Fe began construction in 1868. It engaged in bitter struggles with its rivals, particularly with the Denver and Rio Grande. Both companies wanted to capture the southern Colorado and New Mexico trade. To do this they had to build the famous Raton Pass. The Santa Fe finally gained possession but only after a pitched battle between the rival workers.

Neither railroad thought of building into the sterile country around Leadville until gold and silver were discovered there. Then, of course, both companies tried to cash in. A great battle over possession of the Royal Gorge of the Arkansas River followed, a battle which ended in the law courts. There the Santa Fe lost its claim.

The Southern Pacific (controlled by the Big Four of the Central Pacific) built southeastward from San Francisco toward New Orleans. By 1883 its famous 'sunset route' was in operation.

When the railroad 'mania' began after the Civil War there were 3,272 miles of track west of the Mississippi. By 1890 there were 72,473.

Pullman travel

The first transcontinental, coast to coast, trip to be accomplished without a change of train, was made in the summer of 1870. The trip was sponsored by George Pullman to publicize his newly-invented sleeping and dining cars. Pullman carriages were luxurious affairs with costly up-holstery and beautiful furniture; this particular train included a smoking room, hair-dressing and shaving saloon, and two well-stocked libraries.

All along the route the passengers stared at the wonders of the west about which they had heard so much. They marvelled at the way the Mormons had made the desert bloom. They passed covered wagons still wearily making their slow way west. They saw parties of Indians and herds of buffalo.

Emigrants, of course, could not afford to travel in such luxury. The daily 'emigrant' trains were for them. They were slow and uncomfortable. Yet they made the journey from Omaha to Sacramento in five days – in a covered wagon it often took five months.

All railroads suffered disasters. Boilers blew up; braking

Emigrant travel

and uncoupling were fraught with dangers; timetables were non-existent; head-on collisions were frequent.

In the far west extremes of climate and terrain presented additional hazards. Snow was the worst. Sometimes the snow was so tightly packed that only dynamite would move it. Trains were often stranded for days at a time.

In the spring, floods carried the tracks away. Mud rotted the ties, bridges sagged and rails warped when torrents of melted snow or avalanches swept down the mountainside.

Winter hazards on the plains included herds of buffalo. During blizzards the animals would start to 'drift' in tight herds. If a train were running into a blizzard which obscured the view an engineer might find himself caught in the middle of a herd of half-wild animals before he knew it. Surrounded by thousands of buffalo the train had no choice but to wait until the animals decided to move on.

Prairie fires, plagues of grasshoppers which covered the track and made it slippery, and the destruction of rails and bridges by hostile Indians were also among the dangers facing the travellers on those early western railroads.

A trestle bridge collapsing

As Wells Fargo and other Express companies transferred their business from stage coach to railway, special carriages known as Express or Baggage Cars were added to trains.

On 6 October 1866, two masked men entered the express car of a train on the Ohio and Mississippi line a few miles from Seymoor, Indiana. The bandits overpowered the messenger, opened the safe with his keys and escaped with some $10,000. This was the first recorded train hold-up in the United States.

The most notorious name in railroad robbery is that of Jesse James. His gang's method was to derail the locomotive as it rounded a bend, overcome the train crew, then rob the passengers and the express car. Their first hold up was in 1872 near Adair in Iowa. In the next three years the gang struck many times. It was only when they attempted to rob the First National Bank of Northfield, Minnesota, that the gang was finally broken up. Jesse James was killed by one of his henchmen, Bob Ford, in 1882.

Train robbers flourished throughout the 1870s and '80s. Their decline was due principally to the efforts of the

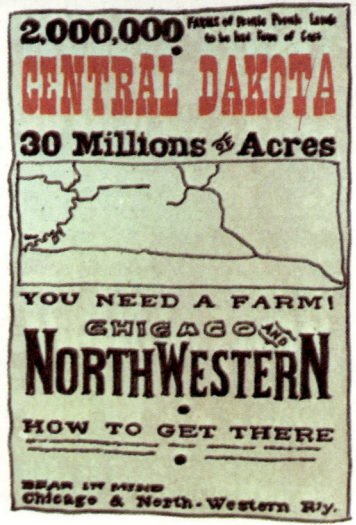

Pinkerton brothers, William and Robert, sons of Allan Pinkerton, the founder of the famous detective agency.

The building of railroads across the plains brought about great economic and social changes. In order to get back some of the vast sums of money they had invested, railroad companies had to sell the land granted them by the government. They embarked on a vast sales campaign not only in the east but also in Europe. The advantages and delights of such states as Kansas, Wyoming, and Nebraska were extolled in glowing terms.

The response was enormous. Special trains were run to bring the settlers to their new homes and small communities of many different nationalities grew up alongside the tracks. The emigrants certainly did not find the land of milk and honey which the railroads had promised them. But because they had nowhere else to go they had to stay – and learn to live in the new land.

Thus, by filling up the last remaining areas of 'free' land the railways virtually abolished the frontier. The problem now was how to fuse the many different cultures and ways of life which had developed in this vast area into one stable society.

CATTLE TRAILS AND COWBOYS

During the decades when Texas was an independent republic and feeling ran high between Mexicans and Texans, most Mexican ranchers abandoned their ranches, and went to live south of the Rio Grande in Mexico.

Texans therefore 'inherited' thousands of 'wild', that is unbranded, cattle. They were all descendents of the animals the Spaniards had brought from Europe but years of living freely on the open plains had changed them into a new breed. Their legs had grown longer enabling them to run from danger and their horns had grown longer and sharper enabling them to beat off attacks from wolves or mountain lions. The Texas 'longhorn', as the new breed was called, was a tough, wiry, resilient creature, as swift as a deer and as sure-footed as a mountain goat.

The Texas Republic declared all unbranded cattle public property. Enterprising Texans, therefore, following the example of the Mexicans, began to round up the longhorns into herds and to put their private brands on them. In fact the Texas cowboy copied the Mexican in all his methods of dealing with cattle. He even adopted the Spaniard's way of dress. By 1845 when Texas became a state of the Union, the Texas cowboy, mounted on a wiry pony, wearing a six-shooter in his belt, a wide-brimmed hat, leather chaparejos and jingling spurs was already a reality. His problem was to find a market for the thousands of longhorned cows by which he was surrounded.

The Nueces Valley: birthplace of the cattle industry

Cowboys home from
the Civil War

In the eastern states and in Europe too, there was at this time a growing demand for hides, hoofs and tallow for the leather and candle industries. But although this trade was flourishing it was too small to be of any great economic significance.

A promising market for beef steers appeared in 1849 when gold was discovered in California. By 1850 some brave ranchers, together with a few hired vaqueros, were gathering a few hundred cattle together, putting them in line and heading for the gold fields. Some got through safely; most met disaster in Arizona and lost their herds and scalps to the Apache Indians.

A small demand for 'beef on the hoof' arose at New Orleans and St Louis but before these markets could be developed the American Civil War broke out. Texas, as part of the Confederacy, sent most of her youth into the fight and for the time being cattle raising had to be forgotten.

At the end of the war Texas was bankrupt. Her veterans, ragged and penniless, returned to their devastated country to find their only assets were the wild herds of longhorned cattle.

In Texas the market value of cattle was three or four dollars a head. In the fast developing victorious north where

there was a great demand for beef, cattle were fetching around thirty or forty dollars a head. How to get his cattle to northern markets became the cattleman's chief pre-occupation during the 1860s.

In 1866 the nearest railway point from which cattle could be shipped north was Sedalia in Missouri. In the spring of that year the first attempts were made to drive Texas cattle from the Nueces Valley to that town, a journey of 1,500 miles.

For most cattlemen the drives were a disaster. There was no established trail to follow. Drovers learnt by trial and error how to get their animals across rivers and deserts. On the Missouri border gangs of armed ruffians, an aftermath of the Civil War, attacked the herds and stampeded them. The excuse given for this dastardly action was that the cows from Texas suffered from a highly infectious fever which had to be kept out of Missouri. But the true motive in most cases, was robbery. Stampeded herds were later rounded up and sold by the Missourians for their own profit.

Putting cattle on to a train in Abilene

Many men lost their lives riding the trails northward; consequently in the spring of 1867 only a few courageous drovers again pointed herds toward Missouri. Their perseverance was to be rewarded, for it was in this year that an Illinois businessman, J. C. McCoy, conceived the idea of establishing a place where the railroad, then pushing west, could meet the cattle trails heading north. His idea was to set up a depot out on the plains to which the Texans, unmolested by border ruffians, could bring their stock, do business with northern and eastern buyers and ship their cattle by rail to any market.

As his point of intersection McCoy chose a cluster of shacks in the middle of nowhere called Abilene. McCoy selected Abilene because, besides being on the route of the Kansas Pacific Railroad, the area was well watered and covered with excellent grass. Thus Abilene became the first cow town; for a while it was a cow town without any cows.

McCoy sent men southward to locate any Texas drovers that might be heading north. The first herd sighted belonged to a man named Thompson. The Texans could hardly believe that a safe and assured market awaited them at Abilene. They feared a trap. Nevertheless they decided to take the risk and headed for the new town. On 5 September 1867, the first cattle were loaded into trucks and transported to Chicago. Texas had found its market.

After 1867 cattle ranching became big business. The drive up to the railroad shipping points became a seasonal occupation. The rest of the year was spent preparing for the long trek north. The work pattern developed into a yearly cycle which began with the annual branding or 'tally' round-up.

On the open ranges where trees are scarce and timber for fencing almost unobtainable no rancher was able to enclose his range. His cattle grazed freely over the grasslands mixing with those of his neighbours. Their only identification was the brand they carried. In the annual spring round-ups, therefore, neighbouring ranchers worked together to sort out their cattle and brand the newly-born calves.

Later in the year came the beef round-up. This time the cowboys collected into one big herd all the cows that carried their boss's brand. From this herd they would select steers most suited for the long trek north; usually two or three years in age and about three thousand in number.

Cutting out a calf from the herd

Longhorns on the trail to the north

As more and more herds were sent up the trail men emerged who had made the journey several times. They became the 'trail bosses'. In every herd, too, a lead steer would emerge – an extra intelligent creature which would automatically take his place at the head of the long line.

Two 'point men' rode alongside the lead steer. The 'swing men' or 'flank men' rode at either side of the herd to prevent rebels from straying outwards. In the rear came the 'drag' consisting of the weak, the footsore and the stragglers. 'Drag men', who had to keep the stragglers moving, rode in a constant cloud of dust. Theirs was the most unwelcome job and was usually given to the rawest recruits.

Every morning, after breakfast, the cook drove his 'chuck wagon' on ahead to the midday camping site. There he prepared a meal for the cowhands to eat as they passed the spot at noon. After clearing away the noonday meal, he went on ahead to prepare the night camp.

The half-wild longhorn was a restless animal. At night it could be panicked by the slightest unexpected noise. Often the dreaded yell 'Stampede!' roused the cowhands from their blankets as the longhorns, startled by a sudden crash of thunder or flash of lightning, began to run in a headstrong

panic-stricken flight towards the distant horizon. Stampedes were the worst hazard of the trails. Many a cowboy lost his life trying to halt those mad rushes of clashing horns and hooves.

Rivers were also a great hazard. In hot weather when the herd was near crazy from thirst they would be dry; in wet weather they could be raging torrents. Other hazards were dust storms and blizzards.

At last, after two or three months of gruelling work on the trail, the cowhands reached the railhead. Then they would be driven into the railway corrals and finally loaded onto the cattle trucks for delivery to the meat-packing factories of Chicago.

After the loading the cowboys were paid off. Yipping and yelling and firing off their six-shooters, they rode into town to clean up and have a good time. The dance halls and saloons were there to help them. Places such as Dodge City became known as the 'Babylon of the Plains'. 'Going on the spree' or 'painting the town red' compensated for the long hours spent in the saddle and the hardships of the trail. All too often the cowhands' hard-earned wages evaporated in two or three days riotous living. Many cowboys headed

Ranch house on the plains

back to Texas as broke as when they started.

Between 1867 and 1885 the great plains area was completely dominated by the cattlemen. Trail drivers discovered that cattle thrived well on the grassy plains north of Red River. The cattleman's frontier, therefore, pushed northward and westward.

Grass and land were free. A would-be rancher simply chose a site as his headquarters, usually alongside a stream and built his ranch house on it. His 'range' was held to cover all the country that his cattle roamed over but he did not own the land. As more and more ranches were established a system of 'range rights' was evolved.

Soon the cattle kingdom extended as far north as Montana and North Dakota through Wyoming, Nebraska, Colorado and Kansas, and westward to New Mexico and Arizona.

The headquarters of the early ranchers of Texas often consisted of no more than a sod shanty or temporary dug-out where they lived just so long as they were branding or rounding-up cattle. When cattle ranching became a full-time occupation ranchers built more permanent homes. These usually started off as simple adobe buildings but as a rancher prospered his home became grander. He added buildings to house his cowhands and his ranch became an almost self-supporting community with blacksmith's shop, dairy, barns and other adjuncts.

One of the largest and most famous ranches was owned by Charles Goodnight. Goodnight served in the army as a scout in the Texas Panhandle before deciding, in 1866, to raise cattle. With his partner Oliver Loving, he drove a herd of cattle across Texas to New Mexico where he set up a ranch on the Pecos River. From here they drove their herds northward to Colorado and blazed a trail which now bears their names: the Goodnight-Loving trail. In 1876, when the Comanches had been driven from the Panhandle, Goodnight set up his headquarters in the Palo Duro Canyon where he built the famous JA Ranch and lived like a feudal baron.

John Chisum was another famous cattle baron. He erected the most luxurious and elaborate ranch in the west. It was situated in the middle of the New Mexican desert. Yet it was surrounded by rose gardens, fruit trees, artificially cultivated woods and sanctuaries of imported birds.

The Chisum ranch

In time the herds beat out certain well-defined highways to the markets. The most used cattle road out of Texas was the Chisholm road or trail. It was named after Jesse Chisholm, half-Scot, half-Indian who, in 1865, drove wagons from Kansas down to the Indian territory to trade with the Indians on the Washita River.

The Panhandle Trail, west of the Chisholm Trail, led up to Kansas and Colorado. The Pecos Trail wound its way up the Pecos River Valley into New Mexico and on to Colorado and Wyoming. As settlers from the east began to move into cattle country and settle along the cattle trails, the cattlemen found it necessary to open up a new trail through the less populated areas some hundred miles west of the old Chisholm Trail. This trail, which ran from San Antonio to Dodge City, was known as the Western Trail.

From Texas the main trails northward diverged after they had passed through Indian territory (now Oklahoma). Some led to the railway shipping points. Others headed due north or north-west. Cattle using these routes were used to

Cattle trails

stock the fast-growing ranges in the territories of Wyoming, Dakota and Montana.

News of huge profits to be made from cattle ranching soon spread abroad. Not only easterners but Englishmen, Scotsmen, Canadians and even Australians flocked to the plains to become ranchers. A little booklet entitled *The Beef Bonanza or How to Get Rich on the Plains*, published in 1881, achieved phenomenal sales in Great Britain. As a result hundreds of British speculators invested their money in the cattle business.

The first large British company to be formed was the Prairie Cattle Company in the Texas Panhandle. Ranching became a fashionable occupation for wealthy young men. English 'milords', French marquises and German barons established a cattleman's 'playground' in Wyoming and Montana. Work on the ranches was supervised by the foremen hired by the companies and syndicates. The owners mostly sat in offices working out their profits.

But in 1885 disaster was at hand. The rush to invest in the

The Hereford or 'Whiteface'

Cattle in a blizzard

west had been so great that the range became overstocked. In the dry summer of 1883 there had not been enough grass for the cattle to live on and thousands had died. Worse was to come.

The summer of 1885 was also a dry, hot one. Prairie fires had played havoc with feeding grounds but by the following December the weather had turned itself inside out. On the night of 31 December from the Dakotas in the north, clean down to Mexico in the south, the greatest blizzard in history struck the plains. Within two days the snow lay so thick that it obliterated all trails and covered all familiar landmarks. The temperature dropped to way below zero. The cold was so fierce that whole families were frozen to death in their cabins.

Thousands of cattle froze to death where they stood. Cowboys sent out to drive them to the more sheltered valleys froze in their saddles. Their horses froze on their feet. Many were not found until the following spring after the thaw had set in.

Never before had there been such a loss of men and stock. Hundreds of ranches were bankrupt and millions of

dollars and cattle lost beyond recovery. Only the concerns owning ranches on the warmer plains of Texas or New Mexico were able to survive.

For years homesteaders or small farmers, had been deterred from setting up farms on the plains because no materials were available to fence in pastures. But in 1873 an Illinois farmer, Joseph Glidden, produced the first length of a new, spiky fencing material. He called it barbed wire. Legend has it that Glidden invented the new wire to keep dogs from trampling over his wife's garden. He had no idea of putting it on the market. Who persuaded Glidden to patent his new fence nobody knows but on 30 December 1879 an advertisement extolling the virtues of barbed wire appeared in the *Galveston News*. Barbed wire was the most important contribution the American industrial revolution ever made to the economy of the cattle industry. It made available a cheap and effective means of enclosing land and was to have an even more far-reaching effect on the development of the plains area.

Emigrant farmers who eagerly bought up the cheap land lots offered by the railways fenced in their homesteads and pastures with barbed wire. Cattlemen, particularly the small ranchers, put up the greatest opposition to the introduction of wire fences. They complained, in many cases justifiably, that their stock would be injured by the sharp spikes of the barbed wire. Cattlemen could only regard farmers, or 'nesters' as they called them, as 'natural' enemies who were encroaching on what had been the rancher's exclusive domain.

The more far-sighted cattlemen adapted to the new conditions. They also bought barbed wire and fenced in as great an area of the land round their ranches as they dared. Often it was not legally their land at all. Only by custom, not by law, did ranchers possess range rights. Small ranchers found themselves cut off from their water supplies by the fences of their richer neighbours. Soon plainsmen were split into two factions: 'fencemen' and 'free range men'.

Masked cowboys cut the wire so that their cattle could

A homestead

pass over a farmer's land. The farmer retaliated by shooting the cattle. Violence, bloodshed, even murder was the result. In the end the fence men triumphed and small ranchers went out of business.

In any case the need for driving cattle long distances to market was coming to an end. As the network of railways spread over the great plains area the character of western ranching changed. The era of the long trails was over. Cattle now needed only to reach the nearest railroad.

Fencing the range also spelled the doom of the longhorn. Now that it was no longer necessary for cattle to walk over a thousand miles to market – a feat which only the tough old longhorns could have accomplished – the cattleman could now breed better, purer stock. In his enclosed pastures he fattened up Durham and Hereford cattle imported from England. As trail tramplers the new breeds were hopelessly weak but as good fat cattle feeding on fenced in ranges they were highly profitable. By 1900 the longhorn, once proud monarch of the plains, was virtually extinct.

A barbed wire cutter

Sheep farmer

Sheep raising began with the Spanish missions and at first was concentrated only in the rugged semi-arid regions of the south-west. As sheepmen sought to move into better grazing lands they came into bitter conflict with the cattlemen. Ranchers claimed that cattle refused to graze on land overrun and closely cropped by sheep. They refused to let shepherds water their flocks and in some areas established 'dead lines' over which sheep could cross only 'on pain of death'.

One of the most famous feuds of the south-west was between the Tewkesbury and Graham families. It began because of the introduction of sheep into Pleasant Valley, Arizona, by one of the Graham brothers. Open warfare continued between the two families for more than five years.

In Wyoming, too, where sheepmen endeavoured to establish themselves on the range during the 1890s, bitter feuds ensued with loss of life on both sides. The famous case of Tom Horn, hanged in Cheyenne in November 1903 as the murderer of Willie Nickell was the result of a cattle versus sheep range war.

THE INDIAN FRONTIER

Anthropologists have grouped North American Indians into seven main cultural areas: Eastern Woodland, South-Eastern Woodland, Plains, Plateau, South-Western, Californian and North-West coast. These cultural areas were split into more than 600 distinct societies which were again divided into hundreds of different groups and tribes

When the white man first crossed the Mississippi the north plains area was dominated by the Blackfeet, Assiniboine and Teton-Dakota (Sioux). To the south lay the hunting grounds of the Crow and the Cheyenne. Further south still were the Kiowa, Comanche, Navaho and Apache. These constituted the main tribes of the Plains Indians' cultural division. They were to prove the white man's fiercest adversaries.

In the mountains and plateaux of the far west lived the Flatheads, Kutenai, Nez Percé, Paiute, Ute, Yakima and other tribes. Those living on the eastern slopes of the mountains had cultures very similar to the Indians of the plains. On the

Plains Indian

plateaux and on the western slopes the tribes led a much more primitive existence.

The most advanced tribes of the area now forming New Mexico and Arizona were the Pueblo people. They lived in permanent dwellings built into the cliffsides of the mesas or in tiers of adobe 'apartment' houses out on the desert. They were a peace-loving docile people and were easily converted to Christianity by the Spanish missionaries from Mexico. The great enemies of the Pueblos were the nomadic and warlike Navahos and Apaches who lived by raiding and hunting.

The most primitive tribes lived in California. Their chief food was the acorn. Their only art was basket weaving. Along the north-west Pacific coast and rivers where food, especially salmon, was abundant, a strikingly different kind of Indian life had developed. Pacific coast Indians built elaborate wooden houses and held great feasts and religious ceremonies. They were a sea-going people. They built huge canoes capable of carrying fifty warriors. They traded and hunted up and down the coast.

Originally, Plains Indians lived in semi-permanent villages situated on the fringes of the prairie. They ventured out into the vast seas of grass only for the annual buffalo hunts which were carried out on foot.

The Spaniards revolutionized plains life by introducing the horse to the Indian. Horses abandoned or lost by the *conquistadores* thrived and multiplied on the plains. By 1684 the Apaches were mounted. Long before the end of the eighteenth century all the Plains Indians could ride. This new mobility enabled them to move out onto the prairie in full force. They became fully nomadic and followed the buffalo herds as they moved south in winter and north in summer. They became expert at firing arrows from horse-back and developed a method of horse-soldiering that kept their Spanish and American enemies at bay for a hundred years.

Warfare amongst the tribes was a kind of bloody game. Bravery in battle counted for more than the slaughter of the enemy. Stealing the enemy's horses was regarded as more honourable than destroying his village. Hunting and fighting

Location of Indian tribes

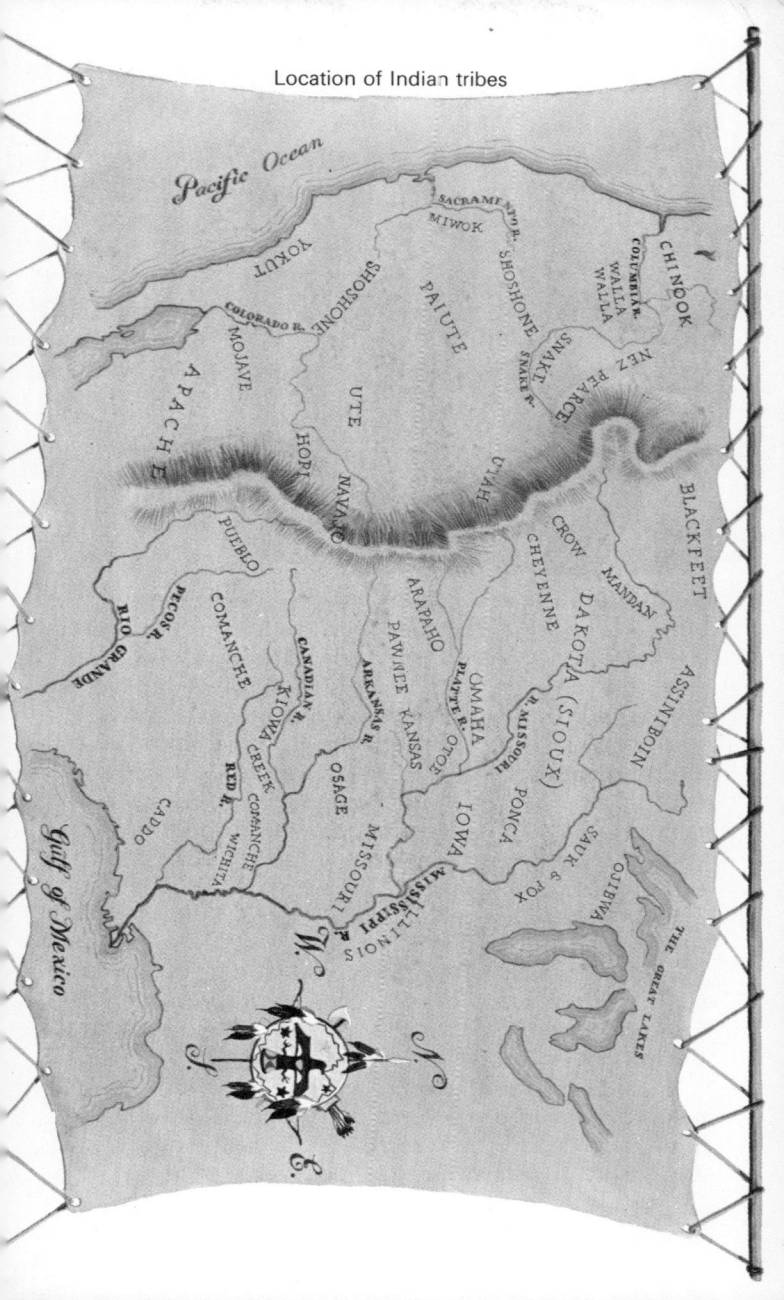

was a way of life. Indian ceremonies, dances, head-dresses, rituals and games, all sprang from the Indians need to hunt the buffalo and to prove themselves brave warriors.

By the time the first wagon trains were heading for Oregon and California the Sioux had become masters of a vast expanse of territory stretching from the Canadian border southward to the Platte River and westward to the Continental Divide. They watched the ever-increasing numbers of white-topped covered wagons with apprehension. They had every sympathy with their allies the Cheyennes who, when they saw the buffalo being driven from their lands, attacked the trains.

Naturally the emigrants retaliated. As tension increased the emigrants demanded protection from the government. A series of army forts was built along the main wagon routes. This was an extra irritant to the Indians who now attacked the forts as well as the wagons.

In 1863 a new trail leading to the newly-discovered goldfields of Montana was opened. It was known as the Bozeman Trail and led straight through the Sioux hunting grounds along the Tongue and the Rosebud rivers.

The average soldier who manned the forts stationed along the wagon trails looked upon all Indians as vermin. Many officers were just and reasonable men who treated Indians as they would other enemies. A few burned with an unreasonable hatred. Lieutenant-Colonel H. M. Chivington was one of these.

The Cheyennes, seeing how hopeless their efforts to stem the white man were, had agreed, in return for the protection of the army – a protection personally guaranteed by the President – to live peacefully within a confined area of the plains. Two of these peaceful Cheyenne tribes, led by their chiefs Black Kettle and White Antelope, set up their winter camp near Fort Lyon in Colorado.

At daybreak on 29 November 1864, Colonel Chivington, incensed by the theft of an army-owned cow, led his troops against this camp. The Indians were alarmed at the soldiers' approach but Black Kettle, knowing he had the protection of the 'Great White Father', ran up the Stars and Stripes over his tepee to show his village was friendly.

Chivington's intentions were far from friendly. He

Sand Creek Massacre – a direct cause of the wars with the Plains Indians

ordered his troops to attack. The warriors scrambled for their weapons, the women and children ran for cover. The Cheyennes put up a stiff fight but after losing seventy-five warriors they were forced to retreat. There were a further 200 casualties among the old men, women and children. Chivington after looting and setting fire to the Indian camp, headed for Denver where he reported he had won a 'great victory'.

Black Kettle carried the news of the treacherous attack to his cousins, the Northern Cheyennes and their allies the Kiowas, the Arapahoes and, above all, to the Dakota Sioux. The Sioux were already angry at the army's decision to run the Bozeman Trail through their territory. News of the Sand Creek massacre inflamed their anger.

The Sioux nation was divided into many separate families or tribes. The principal ones were the Ogallala, the Unkpapa, the Sans Arc, the Brulé and the Minneconjou. Each of these tribes had its own chief and band of warriors. The most powerful chief was Red Cloud of the Ogallala. When he announced his intention of fighting the whites, young

Wagon Box fight

warriors from all the other tribes flocked to join him. The Sioux, the fiercest and most powerful warriors on the plains, rose up to defend their land against the whites.

The great Sioux wars really began on 15 July 1866, when work was started on the first army fort along the disputed Bozeman Trail. The Indians under Red Cloud kept up a constant pressure on the soldiers. Every wagon train arriving or leaving the fort was attacked.

In December Captain William Fetterman pursued a small body of Indians who had attacked a wood train. The captain and his soldiers were decoyed to a level valley out of sight of the fort and there decimated by thousands of warriors.

Almost a year later the same tactics were tried against another wood-gathering party commanded by Captain J. N. Powell. Powell, instead of pursuing the small band of Indians, removed the wheels from his wagons and arranged the remaining 'boxes' in a circle. He ordered his men to take up battle stations within this temporary fort. He then settled down to wait for Red Cloud to attack.

The Indian method of attack was to charge the defenders in frontal waves of cavalry. The first line drew the fire of the single-shot rifles. Before the soldiers had time to reload, the second line of Indians would be upon them. If not the second then the third. Whenever the Indians greatly outnumbered the soldiers this tactic had never failed. So Red Cloud was certain of victory. Instead he suffered a crushing defeat.

The Indians did not know that the soldiers had recently been issued with the new Springfield-Allin rifle which could fire a number of shots in rapid succession. The volley from the soldiers when the second line bore down on them wiped the charging warriors out completely. The third wave suffered the same fate.

Red Cloud, surprised and puzzled by this unusual turn of events, continued to send wave after wave of warriors against the wagon boxes. He lost hundreds of warriors. When strong reinforcements were sighted arriving from Fort Phil Kearney the chief was forced to call a retreat.

The Wagon Box fight was the first decisive victory for the

Fort Phil Kearny put to the torch

Miners in the Black Hills

U.S. Army. However, in the face of such stiff Sioux resistance, the government decided to abandon the Bozeman Trail and to talk peace. Red Cloud was assured that the Powder River country, including the Black Hills, would be ceded to the Sioux for ever. All forts within this area would be abandoned. In August 1868, the soldiers marched out of Fort Phil Kearny. As the last soldiers rode out the Sioux and the Cheyennes rode in and put it to the torch.

After the signing of the 1868 treaty President Grant inaugurated a policy of *peaceful* settlement with the Indians. Missionaries were sent among the tribes. Attempts were made by the Indian Bureau to gather all the Sioux nation into the newly-formed Spotted Tail, Red Cloud and Standing Pine agencies. These attempts were only half successful. Many Indians did go to the reservations in the winter to obtain food and shelter, but in the spring they set off once more for the Black Hills to hunt the buffalo and to live their old, free nomadic life.

The army advocated tougher measures against the 'hostiles', as they chose to call non-reservation Indians, and told the Indian Bureau to get all Sioux into the reserves. Red Cloud knowing the futility of facing repeating rifles and artillery with only lances and arrows, reluctantly advised his warriors to go into the reservations. But Chief Sitting Bull of the Unkpapas and Chief Crazy Horse of the Ogallalas continued to roam the sacred hunting grounds and to live in the traditional ways of their forefathers.

In 1874 gold was discovered in the Black Hills. White men began to flock to the area. The government were worried at this deliberate violation of the peace treaty. Then someone had the bright idea of buying the Black Hills from the Sioux. The Indians were offered six million dollars for mining rights. Crazy Horse's reply was short and to the point: 'One does not sell the earth upon which the people walk.'

A conference between Indians and white men

The army urged even stronger measures against the 'hostiles'. In December 1875, the Government *ordered* the Sioux into the reservations. The weather was so cold it was doubtful if any of the 'hostile' Indians could have obeyed the order even had they wanted to. Such a request only showed the Indian what a foolish creature the white man was.

General Terry sent a message to all the tribes that, unless they came into the reservations by 1 January 1876, soldiers would be sent to fetch them. None of the 'hostiles' obeyed.

Before the spring thaw set in, General George Crook with

Right: the army attacking Crazy Horse's village

The great Sioux warrior Crazy Horse leading his warriors

ten cavalry and two infantry companies, headed for Sioux country. Crook intended to strike while the Indians were still in their winter camps. On 17 May, a detachment led by Colonel J. J. Reynolds came upon Crazy Horse's village in the Powder River Valley. It was bitterly cold. Reynolds decided to attack by night when every Indian was snug within his tepee. The soldiers quickly took possession of the camp and of the Indian's whole horse herd. The Indians fled. But Crazy Horse was not defeated. Knowing that without food, clothing and shelter he and his people must freeze to death, Crazy Horse and his warriors launched a counter-attack. The soldiers retreated, driving the horse herd before them.

Horse stealing was something all Indians knew about. When the soldiers camped the next night Crazy Horse and his warriors recaptured the stolen ponies and some army horses as well. Reynolds decided to return to Fort Fetterman and wait for better weather conditions. Crazy Horse had won the first round.

It was June before the army took to the field again. The first objective was to locate the Sioux summer camp. In the rugged terrain there was little or no communication between the various forces. General Cook led the main contingent from Fort Fetterman while General Terry advanced towards Powder River from the east. One of Terry's officers was Colonel George Custer of the 7th Cavalry.

If Crazy Horse was the Sioux's greatest general, Sitting Bull was their greatest politician. In April 1876 he called a great council. It was held on the banks of the Rosebud River.

Many famous chiefs were there including Crazy Horse, Black Moon, Spotted Eagle and Touch the Clouds. Some Northern Cheyenne and Arapahoe chiefs were also present. In June the huge village moved to Ash Creek to observe the annual Sun Dance.

Sitting Bull took part in this gruelling ceremony and danced until he sank unconscious to the ground. When he revived he announced that he had received a powerful prophetic vision. He had seen many white soldiers falling

upside down into an Indian camp. This portent indicated a great victory. The Sioux then moved their camp to the pleasant valley of the Little Big Horn River in Montana.

Meanwhile the trail left by the Sioux had been discovered and the American armies were moving in. General Terry planned to find the village and attack it. Colonel Custer was to lead the 7th Cavalry up the Rosebud until he came upon the reported trail. If he found the village he was not to attack but was to wait for reinforcements.

G. A. Custer

Skirmish between soldiers and the Sioux

Battle of the Little Big Horn, 25 June 1876

To this day the controversy endures as to why Custer disobeyed orders. He knew that Sioux scouts had carried news of the approaching soldiers to Sitting Bull. Possibly Custer felt that, having been discovered, it was best to attack before the Indians could organize and attack *him*.

At noon on 25 June Custer split his force into three. One detachment was sent to circle the southern end of the valley; a second, under Major Reno, was to ride on down the valley and into the village; Custer himself, with five troops, headed north-west up the right bank of the creek to make the main attack from that direction.

As Custer and his men disappeared behind a bluff Reno led his soldiers into the valley. Suddenly hundreds of Indians, led by Crazy Horse, appeared from all directions. Reno was forced to retreat or be annihilated. He managed to withdraw his force across the Little Big Horn River and make a stand among the bluffs on the other side. Half of his men had been killed or wounded. He was fearful of being able to hold his position when, to his relief and amazement, the

Indians suddenly wheeled round and raced back towards the village. They had, in fact, gone to combat Custer's attack from the far end.

Custer probably had no idea of the great number of warriors camped along the Little Big Horn. The red hordes dashed across the river and met the cavalry as they were coming down the hill. With Indians on two sides of him and the river in front Custer was forced to retreat back up the slope. But just before he could reach it more warriors came swarming over the brow of the very hill he was making for. Custer was doomed. Within an hour every man in the contingent had been killed.

Two hundred and six men died with Custer; fifty-seven more in Reno's command. Inspired by Sitting Bull's vision the Sioux had fought with unprecedented determination. His dream of soldiers falling into camp upside down had come true. The next day, having heard from his scouts that large army reinforcements were on the way, Sitting Bull ordered the Sioux to leave the valley.

Crazy Horse

The Sioux had won a great victory but were never able to put up such a united and vigorous resistance again. The following winter lack of game forced the tribes to split up. The white soldiers gave them no peace. The Cheyennes were attacked in their winter camp and forced to surrender. Sitting Bull and his followers fled to Canada. Only Crazy Horse still remained at large. At last, with game scarce and the women and children half frozen and half starved, even he gave up. In February 1877, he agreed to take his people into the Red Cloud Agency. There he was murdered while attempting to take his sick wife to the Spotted Tail Agency for medical treatment.

Sitting Bull remained in Canada until 1890 when the old chief was permitted to return to the States and to live in the agency at Standing Rock.

The Sioux nation was to make one last, desperate effort to free their country from white domination. A strange new religion arose. It started in Nevada where a Paiute claimed to have had a visitation in which the Great Spirit had given him a magic dance to teach to his people. This dance, called the Ghost Dance, rapidly spread from tribe to tribe.

To the Sioux, the message of the Ghost Dance was especially clear; once more they would know their former glories. 'Over the whole earth they are coming, the buffalo

Sitting Bull

are coming . . .' So ran one of their chants accompanying the dance. 'Ghost shirts' were made. The medicine men said they would protect their wearers from all physical harm.

Many Sioux moved out from the Pine Ridge Reservation to the bad lands. The agents feared an Indian outbreak and sent for troops. When Sitting Bull asked for a pass to visit Pine Ridge a detachment of Indian police was sent to arrest him. As he was led from his cabin his followers tried to rescue him. In the ensuing scuffle Sitting Bull was shot dead.

With the death of Sitting Bull tension grew stronger. More Indians moved out of the reserves. The troops were sent to bring them back. At Wounded Knee Creek Colonel Forsyth of the 7th Cavalry found the village and surrounded it. He asked for and received unconditional surrender.

There are conflicting reports as to what happened next. Some say a medicine man called on the Sioux to resist, crying that they would all be protected by their ghost shirts. Others that a soldier fired the first shot. In any case the camp was surrounded by machine-guns and all but a few of the 'hostiles' were mown down in a few minutes. The soldiers of the 7th Cavalry had taken the skirmish as an excuse to avenge the death of Custer.

It was the Sioux's last battle and the last of the Indian wars – at least on the northern plains.

Before the white men came to the west, the buffalo roamed the plains in vast herds. An early visitor estimated that one herd he saw was fifty miles deep and contained at least four million animals. Yet in less than twenty years – from 1865-84 – these creatures were almost wiped out.

With the coming of the railroad the need to feed the construction gangs turned buffalo hunting into a profession. Men such as Buffalo Bill Cody slaughtered literally thousands of the animals. Even greater destruction took place when it was found that buffalo hide made good 'buff'; the leather used for military buff-coat or jerkin. Special depots were established to which hunters could bring the hides and have them shipped to the east. Dodge City in Kansas grew prosperous in this way. By 1872 it was the centre of the industry. By 1873 there wasn't a buffalo left in Kansas.

South of Kansas lay 'Indian Territory'. By the treaty of 1867 no white man was supposed to enter it without the Indians' permission. But the hide hunters had no respect for treaties.

Left: buffalo killers. *Above:* battle of Adobe Walls

Singly, or in small groups they invaded Indian territory in search of buffalo.

The depot to which these illegal hunters brought their hides was an old fur-trading post called Adobe Walls. On the night of 26 June 1874, a war party of Comanches, Kiowas and Southern Cheyennes attacked it. The buffalo hunters met the assault with heavy large-bore buffalo guns which could shoot long distances and were extremely accurate. The warriors were forced to give up the fight after fiercely attacking for three consecutive days. Soon western Kansas, eastern Colorado and the Texas Panhandle were aflame. Settlements, farms and wagon trains were attacked. The full force of the plains army was needed to quell the uprising. Gradually the Indians were forced into the reservations. Meanwhile the buffalo hunters continued their slaughter.

By 1877 there was hardly a buffalo left. Truly, as General Sheridan said in Congress when an attempt was made to stop the destruction: 'The buffalo hunters have done more in two years to settle the vexed Indian question than the entire U.S. army has done in ten.'

It was a sentiment echoed by a vast number of white settlers. In spite of the entreaties of the medicine men to the Great Spirit, the buffalo did not come back.

Apache village

The sun-baked lands of the extreme south-western plains were dominated by the Navahos and the Apaches. In New Mexico and Arizona these two closely-related tribes brought terror to the peaceful Pueblo peoples and to the settlers, mostly Spanish, who tried to enter the territory from Mexico.

The Navahos proved to be very adaptable and developed into a pastoral sheep-rearing people. Their blankets and manual arts have become world-famous. They have the largest population of any single tribe in the west today.

The Apaches, whose very name means 'enemy' refused to change and were the fiercest Indians the white men had to face.

For many years the Apaches were undisturbed. The sandy deserts, rocky canyons and infertile soil of their territory had little attraction for the American settler. Before 1837 the few white traders who had ventured into Apache land suffered little at their hands. But, as always, it was greed that spoiled any chance of peaceful relations developing between these red men and the whites.

Johnson's massacre of the Apaches

The enmity between the Mexicans and the Apaches persisted long after Mexico became independent. The Governor of Chihuahua offered rewards of 100 dollars for the scalp of any Apache warrior, 50 for a squaw and 25 for a child. An unscrupulous white trapper named Jesse Johnson saw in this decree a quick way to make money. In 1822 the Spanish had discovered copper at Santa Rita in New Mexico and by dint of bribery had persuaded the Apache chief, Juan Jose, to let them work it. Jose became fat and lazy on the good food and drink pressed on him by the Spaniards. In return he kept his people from molesting them.

Johnson, aware of the chief's weakness for food and drink, invited him and his followers to a feast in the town. While they were feeling the effects of the free drink the Indians were subjected to murderous shell fire from two howitzers concealed behind a screen of brushwood at the end of the plaza. Only a handful of Apaches escaped. Just as the Sand Creek massacre sparked off the Sioux wars so did Johnson's action provoke the Apaches into bloody revenge.

Mangas Colorado led the Apaches in a war of revenge in New Mexico

Mangas Colorado was exceptionally tall for an Apache. He was blessed with the qualities of a great leader. He vowed to destroy Santa Rita. By uniting all the neighbouring Apache tribes and keeping a constant watch on the only two roads he was able to prevent any men or supplies from entering the settlement.

Johnson and his party decided to leave. When the party of Americans were some miles from the town the Apaches struck. Mangas Colorado himself pursued Johnson. But the man who began the war escaped by the aid of a lucky shot that killed the Apache's horse.

Plague broke out in Santa Rita. When the Mexican community tried to leave they suffered the same fate as the Americans. Of all the people in the town only a priest and a few women and children were allowed to reach Janos in Mexico.

In 1846, after the war with Mexico, Mangas Colorado found his country under American rule. Soon many 'white eyes', as the Apaches called the white men, began to pour into Apache country. Gold, of course, was the lure. Mangas

Colorado tried to persuade the goldseekers to go on to the Chiricahua Mountains where he knew there was gold in plenty. They ignored him. Worse, when he tried to talk to them a second time a group of miners, under guise of friendship, captured him, pinned him to the ground and flogged him.

Henceforward it was war. Mangas Colorado and Cochise, chief of the Chiricahuas joined forces. They attacked Pinos Altos. They wiped out supply trains, poisoned the water supply and killed more than a third of the miners. Troops marching from California to join the Union forces in the Civil War were ambushed. During one of these engagements Mangas Colorado was shot and seriously wounded.

In 1863 Captain E. D. Shirland sent a message under a flag of truce asking Mangas Colorado to visit him. In spite of remonstrances from his followers Mangas Colorado went, hoping to bring peace to his people. Instead, the moment he entered the American camp, he was arrested. 'If he attempts to escape, I want him killed', said Colonel J. R. West to the guards. That night there came the sound of shots. Colonel

Cochise was an Apache leader noted for his courage and military skill

West came running out of his tent. 'Beg to report that the Indian tried to escape, sir', reported the guard, 'We shot him, as ordered.'

President Grant sent Vincent Colyer to talk Cochise into making peace. Colyer succeeded. He persuaded the chief that if he stopped his raids on white settlements he and his people would be allowed to stay in a reservation in the Chiricahua mountains. Cochise accepted, stipulating, however, that *his* followers were never to be sent to the Tularosa Reservation in New Mexico as other Apaches had been.

Colyer promised that this would never happen. But, as with most other white promises to Indians, this promise was not kept. Only a few months later Cochise was ordered to take his people to Tularosa. He rebelled, led his followers into a hiding place in the mountains and went on the war-path.

In July 1871, General George Crook took command in Arizona. He knew the Indians well. They called him Nan-tan Lupan (Chief Gray Wolf). His first move was to form a corps of scouts recruited from friendly Apaches, Navahos, Pueblos and Mexicans. Crook knew that since the death of Mangas Colorado the Apaches had never been united and that much hostility existed between the various tribes. He used this fact to full advantage.

Slowly but surely the hostile groups were hunted down and assigned to reservations. Here, too, Crook inaugurated a new policy. He encouraged the Apaches to cultivate the land and tried to instil a sense of responsibility into the various chiefs. The Apaches, he said, ought to be able to keep order among their own people. In most cases his plan worked and under military supervision the Indians worked hard and happily at learning to be farmers. Cochise surrendered to General Howard, but only on the assurance that his tribe would be allowed to stay in the Chiricahuas. Cochise himself spent the rest of his life peacefully on the reservation in the land of his people. But only eighteen months later the solemn treaty he had made was broken again.

General Crook

Cochise died in 1876. General Crook was transferred to the north to deal with the Sioux. Responsibility for the Indian reservations in Arizona was given to the Department of the Interior. Crook's patient work went for nothing. The Indian Bureau began a policy of 'concentrating' the reservations. One by one the tribes were moved from the mountains down to San Carlos in the hot arid valley of the Gila. Some chiefs managed to avoid the soldiers and join Cochise's people the Chiricahuas. Among them were two Mimbrenos, Victorio and Geronimo.

In April 1879, the Chiricahuas were ordered to San Carlos. Victorio slipped out of the reservation with thirty of his warriors and headed south. From a hiding place high in the mountains he made devastating raids into Texas and New Mexico. He was soon joined by warriors from many different reservations.

For months Victorio terrorized the south-west. He was

Victorio terrorized the south-west

134

killed at last when 2,000 American troops and a company of Mexican police ambushed him in the Tres Castillos mountains in Mexico.

The last and bitterest struggle was with Geronimo. General Crook called him the 'human tiger'. For two years, under an agent appointed by General Crook, the Apaches had lived peacefully at San Carlos. When a new Indian Bureau agent was appointed, Geronimo and his warriors walked out of the reservation. That was in May 1885. General Crook resigned his post in protest at General Sheridan's order that he was to accept only unconditional surrender from Apaches. General Miles was appointed in Crook's place.

For more than a year Miles and 5,000 troops campaigned against Geronimo's tiny band of Apaches. It numbered no more than eighteen warriors and a few women and children. Geronimo felt cornered and as a consequence his raids grew more and more savage.

The press screamed for his arrest. The people trembled at the sound of his name. He

Geronimo raided lonely ranches

The Heliograph

twisted and turned and escaped the soldiers but the the end was near.

General Miles was the first soldier to introduce the heliograph into desert warfare. Morse code signals could be flashed by this device from mountain tops and high rocks. With its aid Miles tightened the net around Geronimo. The soldiers closed in. Finally he received a message through two squaws that Geronimo was ready to surrender. Lieutenant Gatewood and two Indian scouts were sent with a flag of truce to Geronimo's camp. On the morning of 3 September 1886, Geronimo brought his followers in. They met General Miles at a place called Skeleton Canyon and gave themselves up. Apache resistance was at an end.

The Cheyennes who had taken part in the Custer massacre had been sent to a reservation in Indian Territory nearly 1,000 miles to the south. Here, in only two years, the unhealthy climate and the inadequate supplies of food reduced the band of warriors from 235 to 79 and their women and children in proportion.

Dull Knife and Little Wolf, their leaders, knew the only

hope of the tribe's survival lay in returning to the northern plains. One night in 1878 the ragged tepees were struck and the few scraggy ponies gathered. The Cheyennes slipped out of the reservation silent as shadows.

Their escape was not discovered until the following day. Then there began a great man hunt which was to culminate in the whole might of the American army aided by civilians, forts, artillery, railroads and telegraphs all trying to intercept or overtake this handful of half-starved Indians.

The Cheyennes travelled at a steady lope, sometimes covering as much as seventy miles a day. They seemed aware of every trap the soldiers set for them.

Fighting, dodging, scavenging for food, horses and ammunition from lonely settlements and ranches, the Cheyennes finally crossed the South Platte River and entered the Niobrara Hills. Here the two chiefs Dull Knife and Little Wolf split up. Dull Knife, the older chief, believed that the soldiers would let them alone now that they were in their own land. Little Wolf knew better. He and his followers pushed on towards Powder River.

Dull Knife

Dull Knife and his people head for home

Dull Knife surrendered to the army and asked that his people should be sent to the Sioux agency. Instead they were told that they would have to go to Fort Robinson further south. Sullenly the Indians marched to their prison. When they reached the fort the men were searched for weapons. None were found. The soldiers did not know that the women and children had concealed the parts of the dismantled guns about their persons. In the long wooden barracks in which they were confined the Indians set about reassembling the guns.

It was the middle of winter. A message came that the Cheyennes were to be sent back to Indian Territory. Dull Knife refused to go. On 5 January Captain Wessells was ordered to march the Indians to Fort Reno far to the south. He gave the Indians an ultimatum: unless they agreed to go he would deprive them of all fuel, food and water.

For five days death songs sounded from the huts. The Cheyennes, it seemed, were determined to die of cold and hunger rather than give in. Then on 10 January a shot rang out and a sentry fell dead. Dull Knife's pitiable little band

had broken out of the barracks and were making their last bid for freedom.

They set out across the snow with a few warriors forming a rear guard. By morning thirty-seven Indians had been killed and fifty-two wounded. The remainder entrenched themselves in some bluffs. They could not be dislodged even with a twelve-pounder gun. By the time reinforcements could be brought up they had gone.

For six days the chase continued. The Cheyennes' last stand was made in the Hat Creek Bluffs on the morning of 21 January 1879. There, as the troops poured a crashing blast of shells into them, they fought to the last cartridge and the last man.

Little Wolf and his band, meanwhile, had pressed on into the wilderness of Montana. There he spent the winter unmolested. In the spring he met Lieutenant W. P. Clark, known to the Indians as 'White Hat'. Clark had always befriended the Cheyennes. He did so now. Thanks to his intervention Little Wolf and his tiny village were allowed to stay in the north.

SETTLING THE WEST

Even with the tribes safely in the reservations the Indian problem was not solved. There remained the question of how they were to live now that their means of existence, the buffalo, had been exterminated. Tribal life, the Indian Bureau decided, must be broken up. Indians should become ordinary American citizens and be absorbed into the national economy and legislation. In 1887 the Allotment Act was passed. Its aim was to turn Indians from their communal way of life and into individual homesteaders. Indians had no experience of private ownership, money or the capitalist system. Unscrupulous white men took advantage of them at every turn; they were swindled and beggared and finally forced into a state of idleness, with nothing left of their self respect or former nobility.

An 'Indian New Deal' was then inaugurated. It recognized that Indian group life was important. Attempts were made to make the reservations politically and administratively self-governing. All this, however, was not to take place until well into the twentieth century.

South of Kansas lay the 68,000 square miles of 'Indian Territory', inhabited by only 75,000 red men. White settlers cast envious eyes on this rolling, fertile land and began to agitate for the opening of the territory for settlement. The government could not resist the pressure and the land was purchased from the Indians for a considerable sum. The Cherokee Strip, as it was known, was to be divided up among white settlers. As there were more settlers than there was land it was decided that would-be claimants should literally race for the plots. Those who arrived and staked their claims first would be permitted to keep the land.

On 22 April 1889 thousands of families lined up around the borders of the strip, some on horseback, some with buckboards or covered wagons. When the starting gun was fired thousands of land-hungry settlers galloped forward to find and claim a piece of the soil. Hundreds .were disappointed.

The homesteader had to adapt himself to a land without timber and virtually without water. With no wood to

PACIFIC OCEAN

SACRAMENTO R.

COLUMBIA R.

COLORADO R.

MEXICO

Papago

Fort Apache (Apache)

San Carlos (Apache)

Navajo

Hopi

Zuni

Nez Perce

Flathead

Blackfeet

Wind River

Crow (Crow)

Cheyenne (Cheyenne)

Mescalero (Apache)

PECOS R.

RIO GRANDE

CANADIAN R.

RIO R.

ARKANSAS R.

PLATTE R.

MISSOURI R.

Standing Rock

Pine Ridge (Sioux)

Rosebud (Sioux)

CANADA

MISSISSIPPI R.

Gulf of Mexico

L. SUPERIOR

L. MICHIGAN

L. HURON

L. ERIE

L. ONTARIO

INDIAN RESERVATIONS (Areas in Red)

Indian Reservations

build houses his first dwelling place was likely to be a dug-out, literally a hole dug into the side of a hill or bank. 'Sod' houses were a little more elaborate. They were constructed from sections of sod cut from the land and built up into walls with crude frames to hold windows and doors. Lack of timber also meant lack of fuel. Pioneers were forced to burn cow or buffalo dung.

Lack of water was a serious problem. Now that the ranges were fenced in, many ranchers found that their cattle no longer had access to rivers and streams. A solution to the water problem was found in the windmill. Wells were dug and windmills erected over them. With the aid of the almost continuous wind that blows across the prairies the water was pumped to the surface and stored in large tanks.

Western wells were completely different from any found

Water windmills

in the east where the pattern was very similar to those of
Europe. Western wells were too deep to be dug by hand.
They were drilled to a depth of three or four hundred feet,
were seldom more than six inches in diameter and were
lined with sheet iron casting.

The battle against the elements was constant. Hot, dry
winds blew the land to dust; prairie fires blackened whole
counties; plagues of grasshoppers ate up crops; violent hail
storms flattened them. Settlers learned to farm on a much
larger scale. They experimented with irrigation schemes and
'dry farming' in which moisture is conserved under the soil
by special methods of tilling.

But it was the new agricultural machinery that really
transformed western farming. Thousands of acres were
brought under the plough and turned into the vast wheat

Early agricultural engine for
driving threshing machine

belt which stretches across the plains today.

Gold, as we have seen, had a great influence on the development of the American west. The search for it brought the Spaniards there in the first place; its discovery in California linked the continent. Throughout the 1850s there were gold strikes in Arizona, Utah, Colorado, Montana and Idaho. In 1859 came the discovery of the famous Comstock Lode in Nevada. Silver was also discovered in Arizona when in 1879 Ed Shieffelen laid the foundations of Tombstone, probably the most famous town in western history.

At the end of the nineteenth century the 'age of electricity' was creating an enormous demand for copper. Deposits of this metal had been discovered by accident by prospectors looking for gold in Arizona, Utah and Montana. It was also found, in some instances, by soldiers chasing Apaches. The Clifton-Morenci copper field in Arizona was discovered by Union soldiers in 1864. One returned after the war to stake a claim. By 1875 a group of copper magnates were operating on full-scale lines. The largest of all copper mines, the Jackling Wildcat in Utah was also discovered by soldiers. Today this mine at Bingham Canyon produces approximately ten

Copper mining in 1900

per cent of the world's copper supply.

In Nacogdoches County, Texas, oil was discovered by accident in 1867 but its importance was not realized, nor was it exploited until the end of the century. In January 1901, the first 'gusher' spouted its column of black liquid from a well at Beaumont on the Gulf Coast.

The event gave rise to another rush of western immigrants. As the oldtime prospector searched for gold so the 'wild-cat' drilled for oil. Oil towns developed in much the same way as cattle or mining towns. Ramshackle camps swarmed with gamblers and hangers on of all kinds; hastily-formed companies organized shady deals and quick profits.

The rolling grasslands became dotted with black derricks. The names of the wells from which the new wealth was derived paid homage to the cattle industry on which the prosperity of the state had been founded: 'Black Steer', 'Longhorn', 'Black Diamond', 'Comanche Chief'. Towns such as Abilene which had declined with the passing of the cattle trails, boomed once again when oil brought them new prosperity.

An oil derrick

There were many reasons why the west became synonymous with lawlessness. First of all there was the great influx of criminals who headed west to escape justice in other parts of the world. Secondly, in the mining camps, cow and railway towns, special conditions existed which fostered lack of responsibility, drunkenness and other anti-social behaviour. Thirdly, much of the west was developed in the aftermath of the Civil War when bitterness between 'Yankees' and 'Southerners' was still strong.

Inevitably, the first law of the west was the law of the gun. Law as it was practised in the east did not exist but a code of behaviour, sometimes called the 'Code of the West', soon emerged. It was a far greater crime to steal a horse than to kill a man. Even after orthodox law and order had been established, horse stealing in this land, where to put a man afoot meant almost certain death, remained a major, often a capital, crime.

In the cattle country the first instruments of law and order

Saturday night in Dodge City

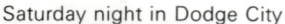

were the Texas Rangers. In the mining districts 'Vigilante Committees' were formed. These first attempts to suppress the lawless elements were crude. 'Vigilantes' did not bother with witnesses, trials or juries. If they considered a man guilty he was hanged. The Montana Vigilantes were especially feared. The mysterious figures 3-7-77 (no one knows what the figures meant) left on the cabin door of a suspected criminal warned him that if he did not clear out he would be visited again and made the central figure of a necktie party.

Inevitably such a system led to injustice. Mob violence and lynchings were prevalent. Personal scores were settled by false accusations. Peaceful citizens wondered who were the worst – the Vigilantes or the renegades.

New communities were organized into 'territories' which were later admitted as states of the Union. Montana became a state in 1889, quickly followed by North and South Dakota, Washington, Idaho and Wyoming. Once statehood

had been granted the land was divided into counties. Sheriffs were elected as law officers for each county; marshals were the police officials of the towns.

Sheriffs and marshals had the power to swear in deputies when needed.

The first peace officers were almost invariably men who were quick on the draw. Only proven gunmen, citizens felt, could cope with the violence of the saloons or the wild antics of the cowboys when they rode into town. So long as efficiency with a gun was the only criterion for marshalship, peace officers tended to be replaced quickly and often. In every town, however, there was a nucleus of honest law-abiding citizens who deplored the violence of the streets. From their ranks emerged peace officers who preferred to bring a criminal to justice to shooting him or hanging him without a trial.

The most famous peace officer was Wyatt Earp. An incident in Ellsworth, Kansas, started him on his career as a peace officer in 1873. The local marshal and county sheriff were powerless to deal with a rowdy bunch of Texas cowboys. Earp had himself sworn in. He stood up to the gang's leader, Ben Thompson and to everyone's amazement, arrested him without a shot being fired. When Marshal of Wichita and later of Dodge, he ordered all Texans to give up their guns when entering town. Having made the decree he enforced it. Although he was an expert gunman he never shot anybody if he could help it. If forced to shoot he shot to kill. He never missed.

His toughest assignment was in the turbulent silver-mining town of Tombstone, Arizona which was dominated and terrorized by the Clanton-McLowery gang. His battle with the gang in the O.K. Corral is probably the most famous gunfight in the world. In the course of the action, which lasted less than a minute, three of the gang were killed.

Cattle ranching produced its own brand of 'bad man': the cattle rustler. In the early days of cattle raising unbranded cattle were considered public property. They could be claimed by anyone who cared to brand them. Rounding up unbranded cattle was known as 'rustling up' and at first the word had no sinister meaning. But later as the range became

Wyatt Earp

Rough justice

more crowded and the 'wild' cattle fewer, cattle 'rustling' became more like cattle 'stealing'. Unscrupulous cowboys could quickly make up herds by sticking their own brand on their employer's calves.

In time, big cattle ranchers suffered so much at the hands of rustlers that they employed bands of armed retainers to protect their herds. This system gave rise to regular cattle wars. One was the Lincoln County War fought between the small ranchers of New Mexico and the cattle 'baron' John Chisum. The Lincoln County War produced Billy the Kid, probably the most famous outlaw of all time. Even when the 'war' was over Billy and his kind did not give up their life of violence.

The Colt revolver, first introduced into the west by the Texas Rangers, became the standard equipment of ranchers, cowboys, peace officers and gunmen of all kinds. The original model underwent many modifications and improvements all aimed at increasing the speed and accuracy of the gun. New types of gun belts and holsters were devised to

Winchester '73

help men to be quick on the draw. Holsters were cut away at the top to expose the trigger and hammer. This allowed the gun to be cocked while being drawn.

Many professional gunmen – both those outside and within the law – practised, often for hours every day. They also experimented with various methods of fast shooting. Some kept the trigger of their weapon permanently tied back with rawhide. This enabled the hammer to be pulled back and released in one movement; the impact against the cartridge being sufficient to 'trigger off' the weapon. 'Fanning' was a method of slapping the open hand against the hammer so that the chamber could be emptied at machine-gun speed.

The most famous Colt revolver was the model known variously as the 'Frontier Model', 'The Peacemaker' and the "73' (it was first issued in that year). It was a .45 single-action, six-shot, model which took centre-fire cartridges and had an effective range of at least 100 yards. In that same year another famous gun appeared – the Winchester repeating rifle.

The word 'Winchester' became synonymous for rifles throughout the west. Guards on stage-coaches carried Winchesters, trains carried a stack of them in the baggage-car as protection against hold-ups; lonely farmers and ranchers kept them handy; Texas Rangers and peace officers carried them. The Winchester '73 was .44 caliber. In 1878 the Colt Peacemaker was rechambered to take the .44 Winchester rifle cartridge. This meant that a man need only carry one kind of ammunition for both his pistol and rifle. The Colt '73 and the Winchester '73 are popularly known as the 'guns that won the west'.

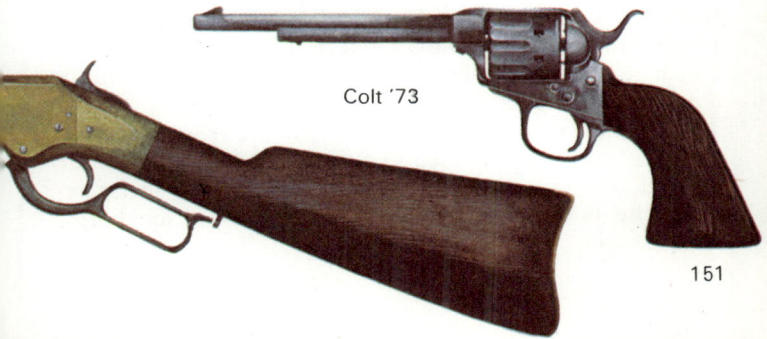

Colt '73

George Catlin

The west has always held a peculiar fascination for writers and artists. One of the earliest visitors was the painter George Catlin. His work entitled *Manners, Customs and Conditions of the North American Indians*, published in 1841, is a most valuable record of Indian life before the encroachment of the white man. Other artists to paint Indians at an early date were Carl Bodmer, who travelled up the Missouri in 1833, and Alfred Jacob Miller who travelled with the Scottish sportsman Sir William Drummond Stewart on a hunting expedition to the Rockies.

The best known western artist is probably Frederick Remington (1861-1909). In 1881 he paid his first visit to Montana. Thenceforward he travelled all over the west, documenting the vanishing frontier. Cowboys at work, Indian fights, army life, prospectors, are all faithfully reproduced in his pictures.

Charles Russell (1864–1926) had no kind of artistic training. Nevertheless, he determined to put on paper a life which he realized was fast disappearing. He immortalized the stampede, the bucking bronco, the great herds of longhorns, the cow camps and the saloons.

Frederick Remington

Authors and journalists also 'discovered' the west. Francis Parkman's *Oregon Trail*, Washington Irving's *Astoria* and Josiah Gregg's *Commerce of the Prairies* are three early contemporary accounts of pioneers, fur traders and the Santa Fe trade.

Andy Adams' *Log of a Cowboy*, published in 1903 is a fascinating, factual account of life along the cattle trails, while Owen Wister's classic *The Virginian* became the first popular novel about cowboy life.

Buffalo Bill Cody was responsible for the birth of the melodramatic 'Wild West' dime novel and magazine. Ned Buntline, a writer of cheap fiction, met the scout during a trip to the west. He made him famous almost overnight with a magazine story entitled *Buffalo Bill, the King of the Border Men*. One of Buntline's stories was dramatized for a New York theatrical presentation. Bill Cody, learning that the public were willing to pay to see someone impersonate him, thought that they would pay more to see him in person, hence he conceived the idea of his 'Wild West Show'. This magnificent spectacle in which real Indians, cowboys, horses and, of course, Buffalo Bill took part, toured the world.

A modern rodeo

The true story of the west is almost as colourful as the dime-novelists painted it. The cult of the 'West' has not been allowed to die. Cattle ranching today may be a more humdrum affair with mechanized equipment to help the cowboys in their job but the wide open spaces, the big hats and the cow ponies are still around. 'Ghost towns' – ruins of former mining camps or trial towns – still exist. In many places their old glories are being restored.

Every year Tombstone holds its 'Helldorado' when its citizens dress up in old-time western costume and re-enact the famous O.K. Corral and other gun battles. The town itself, still looking very much like its old self, is a great tourist attraction.

Rodeos and 'dude' ranches (where visitors can ride the range on real cow ponies) help to keep the legend alive. Indian ceremonials and arts and crafts are also a great draw.

The natural grandeur of the west, its canyons, deserts, waterfalls and mountains are admired by thousands of tourists who visit such places as Grand Canyon, the Painted Desert and Yellowstone National Park. The Black Hills of Dakota are now a holiday camping centre. Mining towns such as Deadwood hold annual 'Frontier Days' celebrations.

The elements remain as fierce as ever. In spite of great irrigation schemes long periods of drought can still bring disaster. In parts of Wyoming it is still not advisable to drive over desolate stretches of road without carrying water. Blizzards create havoc in the winter. Hurricanes strike in the summer.

The west remains a land of contrasts. It is a land of great industrial centres, the glittering world of Hollywood, the affluence of the Texas oil magnates; it is also a land of poverty, especially on Indian reservations.

On the Arizona desert the Apaches have learnt to farm and raise cattle. The Pueblo Indians still live in adobe houses as their forefathers have done for generations. They still raise crops, weave blankets, grind corn, practice rites to promote long life, healing, rainfall and fertility. Alongside the Pueblos on the deserts of Arizona and New Mexico the white men consolidate their conquest with rocket bases and nuclear power stations.

BOOKS TO READ

A History of the American People (2 volumes) by James Truslove Adams (George Routledge & Sons 1943)

The American Pageant by Thomas A. Bailey (D.C. Heath and Co., Boston, 1961)

The Wilderness Trail (2 volumes) by Charles A. Hanna (New York, 1911)

The Winning of the West (6 volumes) by Theodore Roosevelt (New York, 1905)

The Journals of Lewis and Clark, edited by Bernard De Voto (Boston, 1953)

Lost Pathfinder (*Zebulon Pike*) by Eugene W. Holland (University of Oklahoma Press, Norman, 1949)

Steamboats of the Western Rivers by Louis T. Hunter (Cambridge Press, Mass, 1949)

Texas, the Lone Star State by N. L. Richardson (New York, 1943)

Commerce of the Prairies (*Santa Fe Trail*) by Max L. Moorehead (edited Josiah Gregg) (University of Oklahoma Press, 1954)

Across the Wide Missouri by Bernard De Voto (Cambridge Press, Mass., 1947)

Bent's Fort by David Lavender (New York, 1955)

Letters and Notes of the Manners, Customs and Conditions of the North American Indians (2 volumes) by George Catlin (London, 1842)

The Texas Rangers by Walter Prescott Webb (New York, 1933)

The Great Plains by Walter Prescott Webb (Ginn and Company 1931)

The Oregon Trail by Francis Parkman (New York, 1911)

The Year of Decision by Bernard De Voto (Boston, 1943)

Gold Rush Album by Joseph H. Jackson (New York, 1949)

The Log of a Cowboy by Andy Adams (New York, 1931)

A Texas Cowboy by Frank Dobie (New York, 1950)

Roughing it in the West by Samuel L. Clemens (Mark Twain), 1872

The Story of Western Railroads by Robert Riegel (New York, 1926)

A Treasury of American Folklore by B. A. Botkin (New York, 1944)

Red Cloud's Folk, a History of the Ogallala Sioux Indians by George Hyde (University of Oklahoma Press, 1937)

Fighting Indians of the West by Martin F. Schmitt and Dee Brown, (New York, 1948)

INDEX

SOME OTHER TITLES IN THIS SERIES

Natural History

The Animal Kingdom
Australian Animals
Bird Behaviour
Birds of Prey
Fishes of the World
Fossil Man
A Guide to the Seashore
Life in the Sea
Mammals of the World
Natural History Collecting
The Plant Kingdom
Prehistoric Animals
Snakes of the World
Wild Cats

Gardening

Chrysanthemums
Garden Flowers
Garden Shrubs
Roses

Popular Science

Atomic Energy
Computers at Work
Electronics
Mathematics
Microscopes & Microscopic Life
The Weather

Arts

Architecture
Jewellery
Porcelain
Victoriana

General Information

Flags
Military Uniforms
Rockets & Missiles
Sailing
Sailing Ships & Sailing Craft
Sea Fishing
Trains

Domestic Animals and Pets

Budgerigars
Cats
Dogs
Horses & Ponies
Pets for Children

Domestic Science

Flower Arranging

History & Mythology

Discovery of
  Africa
  North America
  Japan
Myths & Legends of
  Ancient Egypt
  Ancient Greece
  The South Seas